DISCARD

THE BEST OF
FRANK

About *Frank*

Frank is Canada's national news and satire magazine, a bi-weekly publication which began life in Halifax in 1987. Published in Ottawa, Halifax and Toronto, *Frank*, circulation 18,000 — is the ultimate insiders' insider guide.

Frank tells the stories that the mainstream media have neither the courage nor the proclivity to print. *Frank* exposes corruption, seeks dirt in high places, and makes Canada's equestrian class uneasy in the saddle.

After all, Canada's establishment elite know so much about us, isn't it time we found out something about them?

For satire, gossip, news, information and humour, there is no publication in North America like *Frank*.

Subscribe today and get the *whole* story.

Perhaps the greatest praise comes from *Frank's* #1 fan, former prime minister Byron Muldoon, "If I could get hold of the editor of *Frank*, I would shoot him."

For more information:

Phone: 1-800-56-FRANK
Or write: Box 604, Halifax,
          Nova Scotia, B3J 2R7

THE BEST OF
FRANK

Four Years of Exposing the Guilty, Provoking the Greedy, and Mocking the Powerful

Michael Bate, Editor

Random House of Canada
Toronto, New York, London, Sydney, Auckland

Dedicated to the memory of Barry Torno and Ron Dann

Published in 1993 by Random House of Canada Limited.

Canadian Cataloguing in Publication Data

The Best of Frank: four years of exposing the guilty, provoking the greedy, and
      mocking the powerful

ISBN: 0-394-22367-5

1. Ottawa (Ont.) - Humor. 2. Canada - Politics and government - Humor. 3. Nova
Scotia - Humor. 4. Nova Scotia - Politics and government - Humor. 5. Canadian
wit and humor (English).* I. Bate, Michael, 1945-

FC3096.3.B38 1993 971.3'84 C93-094044-X
F1059.5.09B38 1993

Printed and bound in Canada
10 9 8 7 6 5 4 3 2 1

Cover photo: Canada Wide / Mike Cassese

FOREWORD

A few years back, just after my partner Kurt Andersen (like me, a refugee from *Time*) and I had started *Spy*, I was asked if the same sort of rude, satirical magazine could be started in Canada. I said no, for any number of reasons, not the least of them being that Canadians weren't as prone to parading around in the over-the-top manner that the run-of-the-mill New York tycoon or politician did in those years. The collection you have in your hands is ample proof of how very wrong I was.

I manage to get my hands on a copy of *Frank* only every other month or so, and the editor recently told a *Washington Post* reporter that I owed the magazine money for some back issues I ordered years ago. These impediments to full enjoyment aside (the editors should invoice me, by the way - I will pay by return mail), I must say that I am in awe of *Frank's* editors and of the suitably grubby magazine they produce with alarming quality every fortnight.

Journalism is not the highest of callings. Indeed the public places journalists just slightly below lawyers and just slightly ahead of serial killers in the social order. Nor is the journalist's lot an easy one. To assemble a reasonable approximation of the truth from a puzzle of disparate bits of information is a daunting task. To do it with lawyers and editors hovering at each shoulder and on deadline is downright hair-raising. The satirist, remember, must do all of this too. And then he must make it funny.

Furthermore, it becomes increasingly difficult to keep ahead of reality. Politicians especially seem to be more corrupt, buffoonish, grovelling and vainglorious than the parody that any satirist could muster.

For satire to really work, it must be on target. An accurate report may sting the victim more, but he is more likely to get on with his life after the hit than if it is inaccurate. An off-target story often leads to the four stages of satirical victimization: anger, denial, revenge and finally, libel representation.

That satire is alive at all these days is a wonder. Canada and the U.S. are in the midst of a comedy epidemic, and comedy, with its bare brick wall backdrop and its toothless verities on growing up Catholic or Jewish or the rigors of dating or being married, is far down the food chain from satire. Satire involves varying proportions of muckraking, irony, commentary and stylish writing. Satire additionally involves attacking the powerful in one form or another. Bite the ankle of the overdog as we used to say at *Spy*!. H.L.

Mencken put it better: afflict the comfortable and comfort the afflicted. And as opposed to being an arm of the press relations industry, which invloves getting things into print that people want, good journalism, and therefore good satire, involves getting things into print that people don't want printed. In a speech he gave a few years back on satire in journalism, A.N. Wilson addressed the notion put forward that "those who object to the destructive power of satire...can only do so from the point of view that politicians deserve to be protected from attack, however corrupt, dangerous or silly they may be."

The result of successful satire is robust sales and social banishment. When the satire is directed toward a woman, the instigator of the attack is branded a misogynist; if it is against a black person, he is a racist; if it is against a Jew, an anti-Semite. And so forth. It gets worse. William Cobbett, in his 19th century monograph *Political Register*, was jailed for his repeated and scabrous attacks on the Army. More recently, Richard Ingrams, editor of *Private Eye*, found himself at the nasty end of a criminal libel action waged by Sir James Goldsmith during Britain's infamous "Goldenballs" trial. A few steps up from everyday libel, a conviction of criminal libel would have sent Ingrams to a jail cell.

Misery of this sort likes company and so I suppose that it is no coincidence that *Frank* is the result of a pair of minds rather than just one. Hilaire Belloc and G.K. Chesterton collaborated on *The Eye Witness*, Mencken and George Jean Nathan on *The American Mercury* and *The Smart Set* and Richard Ingrams and Paul Foot were the two integral founders of *Private Eye*. *Spy* also was a thorough collaboration of its two founding editors.

The tradition of the satirical journal is as old as modern governance. Orwell, Wilde, Pope and Swift all swam in the waters of satire and its eddy pool, muckraking. For many of us, our lasting impressions of 18th and 19th century politicians and businessmen we owe to the satirical sketches of Hogarth, Cruikshank, Gillray, Rowlandson and Daumier.

Canada, so long a petri dish for American popular humour, was home of course to Stephen Leacock, a seminal satirist whose work inspired George Ade and S.J. Perelman. And they in turn inspired almost every comic writer who succeeded them. The current health of satire in Canada is evidenced not only by *Frank*, but by the success of *The Royal Canadian Air Farce* and the huge influences of *Second City* and *Saturday Night Live*.

It is, of course, horrible to be written about in a magazine like Frank. To the victims, and I know this is scant comfort, I say that to be written about is unpleasant, but to not be written about at all is far worse. We tend to kid the ones we love. And in the same vein, the satirist often feels a grudging respect and fascination for his subject. I have long felt that Richard Ingrams and Jimmy Goldsmith, who have been at each other's throats in print and in the libel courts for two decades, would actually enjoy the other's company were they to sit down over lunch on some neutral territory. I confess to being fascinated and at times admiring of our own chief characters: short-fingered vulgarian, Donald Trump; CAA chairman, Mike "The Manipulator" Ovitz; and former *New York Times* executive editor, Abe "I'm writing as bad as I can " Rosenthal.

I have been out of Canada too long to know precisely what the reaction is each time an issue of *Frank* hits the stands. Those written about, I suspect, fling the copy into the wastebasket, and those spared recline for a decent entertainment at someone else's expense. The one targeted for abuse should remember that the more comfortable and confident a person is with themself, the more easily they are able to brush off the effects of criticism or ribbing. Similarly, the health of a country is in direct proportion to its ability to laugh at itself. Satire and how it is received is a vitally accurate measure of a nation's strength and self-knowledge. The quality and success of *Frank* is, in its way, a direct compliment to Canada.

Graydon Carter
New York City
July 1993

INTRODUCTION

Those who want to rebuild the world and those who want to laugh at it are frequently at odds.

–Patrick Marnham

My first encounter with David Bentley was in November 1989. We met at a deli on Sparks Street, near Parliament Hill. Bentley reminded me of Wemmick in *Great Expectations*. Engaging, energetic, with a keen eye for hypocrisy and pomposity, this Dickensian character quickly sold me on the notion that we could make a success of a magazine along the lines of Britains's *Private Eye*.

Bentley had established the first *Frank* in Halifax in 1987 with co-founders Lyndon Watkins and Dulcie Conrad. I shared their passions for satire and humour, and for a publication that told the whole story, not the laundered account of events we get in the daily press. Convinced there was an audience as frustrated as we were with the politically correct, bland and predictable institutional information the mainstream media serve up, we created Ottawa *Frank*.

We never had a business plan or conducted any market research that told us *Frank* could work. On the contrary, nearly everyone told us it was doomed to fail. Graydon Carter, John Fraser, Auberon Waugh, and others we spoke to were skeptical. Not enough celebrities in Canada, they said. Canada lacks an entertainment industry. We're a dull, third-rate country of no interest to anyone, least of all ourselves, After all, look what happened to *Zed*, the satirical magazine launched in 1985. *Zed* had a quarter of a million dollars behind it and never reached the stands. *Yorker*, the Toronto satirical monthly, published three issues and folded in 1987.

Thus, *Frank*, a seat-of-the-pants idea run by amateurs, set out to establish a Canadian news and satire magazine that would be independently distributed and circulation-driven. This antidote to the mainstream press would function on a shoestring budget: cheap and cheerful on low-grade newsprint. Somehow, this was going to be accomplished with no advertising, no government grants, no promotion, no direct mail campaign, no money, and no staff to speak of (we have two full-time employees at Ottawa *Frank*).

As I soon discovered, such a magazine has many benefits, chief among them its simplicity. "Keep things informal and cheap," said Patrick Marnham, "and one can avoid the great constraints of freedom which adult life often imposes." I also learned quickly that writing and editing *Frank* is a liberating experience. By its very nature, *Frank* is direct, to the point. We don't worry too much about things like lawsuits, bad taste, or "going too far."

Of course, not everyone shares our enthusiasm for anarchy. Former prime minister Byron Muldoon described *Frank* as a "vile…trash magazine." Another great Canadian, Sondra Gotlieb, rates us as "tasteless and disgusting." Ah, yes, good taste, that subtle protection for Canada's equestrian class.

Contrary to the mainstream media, in their quest for stories based only on confirmed facts, Frank starts with the assummption that most important news stories start their lives as rumour. We verify and fact check like any other news publication. But at Frank we also take risks. We print stories without the smoking gun. Because who sets the limits on which stories get told? No doubt the equestrian class, big business and politicians. Personally, I'd rather have it out there where I can see it and make up my own mind than have someone decide for me.

We have often been the prey of the politically correct, who seem to have a penchant for making hate calls to our office, threatening us with laswuits, and generally thinking it would be more democratic to have us shut down. Ironically, the most complimentary words came from our former prime minister, who said he would shoot us himself, given half the chance.

Since the beginning of *Frank* there has always been much confusion over the satire in the magazine. Where do the jokes begin and end? Tony Hendra, a founder of *National Lampoon*, described satire as "intellectual judo, in which the writer takes on the ideas and character of his target and then takes both to absurd lengths to destroy them." The uninitiated have often accused *Frank* of sharing our targets' beliefs. What is real and what is not? I can only suggest readers make up their own minds. Perhaps this collection of our best lampoons, cartoon, parodies and satire from the past four years will help them figure it out. Maybe not. After all, nothing is certain: the ambiguity is often best left in the box.

Like any attempt to capture history on the run, this collection includes items that time has since passed by. Just think of the book as representing a slice of the past four years, for better or worse, or just plain funny.

My thanks to the principal contributors who were reckless enough to put their names to it: Glen McGregor, Geoff Heinricks, Charles Jaffe, Terry Mosher, and Harry Spilman. Thanks also to David Bentley, Doug Pepper and Will McDowell. And most of all, to Dijana, who never wavered.

Michael Bate
July 1993

THE MULDOON YEARS

"I think I just trickled down my own leg, son."

"That was my leg... Dad?"

Mr. Prime Minister, could you move your arms, please?   Thank-you.

To Ceaucescus: "Hey, come on fellows, put those rifles down. I only dropped by to pick up a cup of sugar."

"I'm A Soul Man!"

God, I was drunker than I thought!

"Show Boat" Muldoon fails to win Third World support for U.N. job.
(Nov. outline 1991)

Excerpts from
Muldoon's Last Tape

First performed on the CBC-TV program *Contact,* March 11, 1992.

Cast of Characters

Imelda Muldoon. Long-suffering shopaholic wife of the punch-drunk prime minister of a fading and divided mid-level Western nation. Despite severe misgivings about how her increasingly defensive and angry husband will comport himself on national television, she is nevertheless supremely confident that her own hair and legs look fabulous.

Hana Gartner. Veteran TV hostess facing the biggest interview of her career. Often wonders how life might have been different had she been named Barbara: like the Barbara at the CBC in whose dark shadow she toils, like the Barbara at ABC with the speech defect. Tonight she will attempt to emerge from the penumbra of the first Barbara by striving to emulate the second. For Hana this ultimate test of media mettle is unexpectedly compounded by a gut-roiling bout of Mexican turista as potentially explosive as Popocatepetl. She is loopy on Kaopectate.

Byron Muldoon. Vulgar, bone-weary political hack nearing the end of a long, ugly career. His fate, too, rests on the outcome of tonight's interview. He knows this may be his final chance to impress the proletariat with what a warm, caring human being he really is, despite all the lies and falsehoods heaped upon him by the extreme left-wing cabal that secretly controls the mass media. He knows he must appear calm and statesmanlike; he must at least pretend that he accepts some of the responsibility for the crassly stupid government he heads; he must turn the other cheek; he must refrain from the life-long compulsion, born of an ineradicable, and thoroughly justified inferiority complex, to exaggerate the slights against him, real or imagined. Tonight he must keep himself in check or all is lost. To this end, he has been painstakingly prepped and prodded by his political cut men. They are a resigned group. They know they can no longer contain the boss's chronic turista of the soul.

IMELDA *(MAKES HER STAGED ENTRANCE AND GREETS HANA)*: How are you? Nice to see you. *(REMINDS HER GUEST WHAT STANDARDS OF SYCOPHANCY ARE EXPECTED OF HER, SHOULD SHE EVER WISH TO BE INVITED BACK)*. Last time I saw you, you were here with Mike Duffy.

HANA *(HOPING IMELDA WON'T THINK IT WAS SHE WHO HOOVERED ALL THE CANAPES AND BROKE THE ANTIQUE CHAIR)*: You remember? *(FEARING HER JOURNALISTIC CREDIBILITY IS SHOT BEFORE THE INTERVIEW HAS EVEN BEGUN)* What an extraordinary memory.

* * *

HANA: I'm curious which of you has the thicker skin?...

IMELDA *(UNABLE TO REMEMBER HOW THAT BUFFOON SEGAL BRIEFED HER ON THIS ONE)*: I don't know how to answer that question.

BYRON *(HALF-HEARTEDLY EMBARKING ON THE CROW-EATING GAME PLAN DEVISED BY HIS HANDLERS)*: I think that Mila has a much healthier outlook for example, in respect of criticism. It took me a lot longer to get used to the attacks on the family and the children and ourselves.

HANA *(SLIPS INTO THE BARBARA WALTERS MODE SHE'S BEEN PRACTICING ON THE TOILET EVER SINCE SHE GOT BACK FROM MEXICO)*: How do you deal with dropping as low as 11 per cent in the polls, which makes you the most unpopular prime minister since the invention of polling?

IMELDA *(SUDDENLY REMINDED OF HER IMPERILLED FIRST-LADY STATUS)*: But 41 per cent undecided, so, I mean, you know...

IMELDA (*UNABLE TO REMEMBER WHO'S SUPPOSED TO BE GOOD COP ON THIS PARTICULAR BEAT*): He's enormously tolerant, he's much more tolerant than I am. And he has a tremendous sense of humour (*TRIES HARD NOT TO THINK ABOUT BYRON'S TIRESOME STABLE OF PRIEST-MINISTER-RABBI JOKES*), so when he comes home he really can leave a lot of it behind in the office. I'm sure that there are moments when he doesn't want to. But I'll tell you something, when he comes in here and there's four children all, each with their own itin-, venues and their own problems and their own interests and their friends running around the house, (*FORGETS WHAT SHE'S TALKING ABOUT*) uh, it puts it on a different plane...

BYRON (*TRYING TO APPEAR PHILOSOPHICAL*): And life brings its own perspective...And so you build your own life irrespective of the criticism.

HANA (*TRIES TO IMAGINE HOW BARBARA W. WOULD HANDLE THE FEELING THAT HER BOWELS WERE ABOUT TO EXPLODE*): But does some criticism cut clear to the bone? When you are accused of selling out your own country, of riding the coattails of the United States? Do you take that personally?

BYRON (*WITH THE SHIT-EATING GRIN OF A MAN WHOSE GAME PLAN DENIES THE VERY ESSENCE OF HIS BEING*): Oh, of course not. (*BUT UNABLE TO RESIST A FEEBLE COUNTERJAB*) That's the pathetic stuff of the extreme left wing in Canada.

* * *

HANA (*INELUCTABLY SLIPPING INTO FRUMSPEAK*) People are very mad at you, Prime Minister. And people are hurting. That 1.5 million out of work, they're angry at GST, they're angry with free trade, they're angry at the recession, they are blaming you. (*EVEN MORE FRUMILY*) What can you say to these people who are hurting you so much?

BYRON (*STRAINING TO STICK TO THE GAME PLAN*): But that's the way it should be. I mean, who do you blame in a democracy? Who do you blame in a democracy, (*REMEMBERS THE TATTERED TORY SHIBBOLETH*) when you're coming out of a difficult recession?

HANA (*SUDDENLY BUOYED BY THE FEELING OF BEING IN CHARGE, SHE SWIFTLY CHANGES GEARS*): Is he warmer and funnier at home?

IMELDA: Oh! Warmer and funny?

BYRON: Ha, ha, ha. It all depends on the heat. Ha, ha.

HANA: Ha (*SUDDENLY REALIZING THE FEELING OF BUOYANCY SHE'S EXPERIENCING IS ACTUALLY A MIASMIC OCCURRENCE OF THE NETHER REGIONS*), ha.

IMELDA: Ahh!

BYRON: If I, if I showed your viewers you through 8.6-second clips, if all, if they didn't see *Hannah* Gartner in 15-minute, uh, demonstrations on television or half hours, they'd have quite a different perception of you.

HANA (*TICKED OFF OVER HIS PRONUNCIATION OF HER NAME*): They wouldn't like me either? (*LAUGHS*)

BYRON: Well, they'd change their opinion of you, obviously. You'd start with a 50 per cent approval rating and you'd work your way down. (*HIS THIN, PARCHED LIPS FORM ANOTHER SHIT-EATER IN AN ATTEMPT TO DISPEL THE NOTION HE'S BLAMING THE MEDIA AGAIN*) And that's what happens to us.

HANA: What are the qualities about (*MISPRONOUNCING HIS NAME*) Brian Mulroney that you find most annoying?

IMELDA (*HER HEART SUDDENLY FILLED WITH THE RESIDUAL PAIN OF HIS MOODS AND HIS INFIDELITIES AND HIS DRINKING*) Annoying?

HANA: Irksome.

IMELDA: Annoying??

HANA (*REALIZING THAT IF THIS WOMAN EVER GETS ROLLING, THEY'LL BE HERE ALL NIGHT*): Not all of them, just some of them.

IMELDA (*WONDERING HOW SHE CAN EVEN BEGIN TO ANSWER THE QUESTION*): ... I wouldn't say annoying....He's really been, I'm overwhelmed sometimes how well he's handled it because he has so much responsibility. The know, the coach of the team...

HANA: But something must get on your nerves. Is he a neatnik, is he a slob?

IMELDA: Uh, he tends to be a little messy (*LAUGHS UPROARIOUSLY*)...

BYRON (*LIMPLY TAKES HOLD OF ANOTHER UNWELCOMED OPPORTUNITY TO BE SELF-DEPRECATING*): All right, all right, "slob"...

IMELDA: He's been, he was in boarding school from the age of 12, till he...

BYRON (*FEELING, AT THE MENTION OF "BOARDING SCHOOL," THAT OLD FAMILIAR ACHE OF REJECTION WELL UP IN HIM*): ...

HANA: So this is a little rebellion now.

IMELDA (*GUESTIMATING HOW MANY HUNDREDS OF TIMES SHE'S NAGGED HIM TO PICK HIS DIRTY UNDERWEAR OFF THE FLOOR SO THE SERVANTS WON'T SEE*): I think there's a certain time when he wasn't terribly tidy. So I think we've brought him down to the halfway point.

* * *

BYRON: We've given up long ago trying to separate fact from fiction. We just let it sit there. There's nothing you can do. You can't challenge it, you can't correct it.

IMELDA: Because you draw much more attention to it...

BYRON: Look, a guy writes a book about us. He's never met Mila, he's never met me, he's never talked to us, and yet he's fabricating conversations that we are alleged to have had, Mila and me having conversations...

IMELDA (*THINKS SADLY OF HOW MANY FRIENDS AND MINIONS BETRAYED THEM*): And what we thought.

BYRON: And what we were thinking at a given point. (*LAUGHS*)

HANA: ...The unnamed book, John Sawatsky's, did you read it all? Did you read it?

IMELDA: No. No, we didn't read it at all. (*SUPPRESSES A DESIRE TO TOUCH HER NOSE TO SEE IF IT HAS SUDDENLY GROWN BACK TO ITS PRE-RHINOPLASTY DIMENSIONS*) You know, we don't live in a vacuum. There have been experts, -cerpts, and people have told us about it and friends of ours who, uh, bought it and read it said it was funn- (*CATCHES HERSELF*), ironic because they didn't say this or didn't say that. I think it's sad that a book that had so much potential...he never interviewed either Brian or me. (*CONVENIENTLY FORGETTING SAWATSKY'S HALF DOZEN IGNORED REQUESTS FOR INTERVIEWS*) How can he legitimately do an expose on an individual who's been around for 50-odd years and never interview him?...

HANA: But granted, he dredged up some drinking, some encounters with women, failing law school and the Quebec bar exams a couple of times—

IMELDA: But all *that's* fair.

HANA: —But it isn't really malicious.

BYRON: Well, what, what, but, uh...

IMELDA (*DREDGING HER MIND FOR SOME WAY OF EXPRESSING THE IGNOMINITY OF IT ALL*): But it could have been, it could have been about *John Doe*...

BYRON: You ask about, you know, did I lose my temper, do I fly off? Yes, I do. (*ALL HIS PENT-UP RAGE AND HOSTILITY IS SUDDENLY RELEASED IN A GREAT SPASM OF SELF-RIGHTEOUSNESS*) When you have a trash magazine that puts (*SUCCUMBING TO A SUDDEN IMPULSE TO EMBELLISH HIS TALE*) on the cover an incitement to gang-rape my daughter, I wanted to, wanted to, to take a gun and (*HIS BRAIN SQUIRMING LIKE A TOAD*), and go down there and do serious damage to these people. I thought it was, it was awful. It was an outrage what they did. And yet, if you ask me whether I lost my temper, you're bloody right I lost my temper. (*FALLING PREY TO THE PHARAONIC FALLACY, A*

DELUSIONARY STATE OF MIND IN WHICH IT IS ASSUMED THAT ANYONE OF LESS POLITICAL POWER IS IPSO FACTO PHYSICALLY SMALLER) And if I'd had had that little guy within striking distance, I'd ah, I'd a liked to choke him, whoever put that on.

IMELDA (*SOMEWHAT RELIEVED THAT HER HUSBAND'S BOIL HAS BEEN LANCED*): ...We actually, we actually hid it from Caroline for two years, for two weeks. We actually hid it from her, so that she would never actually see. (*SUDDENLY FEELING JUSTIFIED IN HAVING DISPATCHED VARIOUS SERVANTS TO DO HER WHIMS IN ALL KINDS OF NASTY WEATHER*) Because we don't go to the newsstands. So we actually concealed it from her...

BYRON (*TRYING HARD TO IGNORE THE FACES OF COATES AND CROSBIE AND KEMPLING AND ALL THE REST OF THE TORY SEXUAL REARGUARD AS THEY DRIFT MOCKINGLY THROUGH HIS MIND'S EYE*): That's the thing that drives me bananas, the insulting offensive thing against women generally. It happened, however, to be against women generally, (*LOPPING A YEAR OFF HIS DAUGHTER'S AGE TO FURTHER FUEL HIS OWN RAGE*) but also against a 16-year-old girl. And this was an incitement to gang-rape my daughter because...

IMELDA: And celebrate the fact. (*LAUGHS*)

BYRON: And celebrate that fact. And some of these columnists (*FUMING OVER THE BETRAYAL BY FOTHERINGHAM AND ALL THE REST OF THESE HACKS WHOSE PECKERS HE ONCE THOUGHT WERE SECURELY IN HIS POCKET*) ...thought it was cute. They actually wrote what an interesting piece of—

IMELDA (*REMEMBERING THE WORD FROM HER BRIEFING NOTES, BURBLES PROUDLY*): Satire—

BYRON: —of satire this was.

IMELDA: I didn't find that theme funny. Just like satire should know that theme of rape, there's no way it can be funny...And therefore I can't understand people who approach it from that basis.

HANA (*THINKING BIG CLOSER AND A QUICK SPRINT TO THE CAN*): Prime Minister, I have to ask you, are you going to come back like Rocky fighting in another sequel?

BYRON: I've come back twice to win general elections and I think that to complete the triumvirate, I should try to do it again. Ha, ha. (*HE SMILES WITH ALL THE BRAVADO HE CAN SUMMON TO TRY TO HIDE THE FACT THAT, AMONG THE MANY, MANY THINGS HE DOES NOT KNOW, HE DOES NOT KNOW WHAT TRIUMVIRATE MEANS*).

— CURTAIN —

24 SUSSEX ROYAL BOUDOIR

FASHION FUN IN PLASTIC SURGERY

1) Cut out designer surgical gown
2) Mix and match faces
3) Visit cosmetic surgeon

Small mouth-big eyes

Big mouth--no eyes

The Julia Roberts/Madonna combo

The Caroline

The Tina Turner

The Marie Antoinette

The Jackson

CANADA POST IN POLE POSITION $2.00

LOBBYISTS OF DEATH — INSIDE THE WESTRAY MINE DISASTER

FRANK

FROM FRUMPY...

...TO FANTASTIC

McLAUGHLIN'S MAKEOVER

Totally gratuitous T&A cover,
Vaguely related story, PAGE 6

JOE BORRELL • OVIDE MERCREDI • MORE TOPLESS GIRLS $2.00

FRANK

ROSEDALE MP'S DIVORCE DRAMA

BARBARELLA AMIEL IN VANITY FAIR?!

Smile, Joe!

TAKE A REST LET WOMEN BARE THEIR CHEST

Topless, leaderless, hopeless...

THE BIGGEST BOOBS on PARLIAMENT HILL

AUGUST 20, 1992 • ISSUE 122 • EVERY TWO WEEKS

FRANK BY NAME, FRANK BY NATURE

FRANK

$2.00
april 18, 1991
every two weeks
issue 87
central canada edition

♪ I feel good. I knew that I would now...♪

Chretien is back!

PRIME TIME SNOREFEST • BABY SENATOR'S BABY $2.00

FRANK

DOUG CREIGHTON'S CRASH AND BURN

BOB RAE GET BOMBE

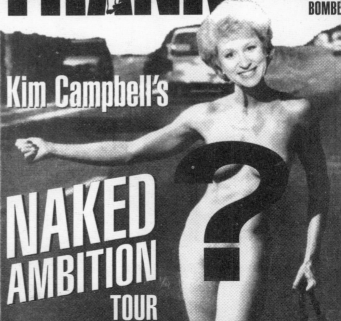

Kim Campbell's

NAKED AMBITION TOUR

NOVEMBER 26, 1992 • ISSUE 129 • EVERY TWO WEEKS

SEXUAL HARASSMENT AT THE GLOBE

$2.00

FRANK

CORPSE

TRUDEAU: I'M STILL DEAD

SAY "NO" TO CRYOGENICS

OCTOBER 15, 1992 • ISSUE 126 • EVERY TWO WEEKS

TAXING BYRON & IMELDA MULDOON

$2.00

FOREST HILL MELTDOWN

FRANK

Hokay, I'm ready. Drop da puck.

Canadian Sports Illustrated

PLAYOFF PREVIEW

APRIL 29, 1993 • ISSUE 140 • EVERY TWO WEEKS

PLUS RALPH BENMERGUI AXED

CARL MASTERS

SOUVENIR TORY LEADERSHIP ISSUE

$2.00

SATURDAY *night* supplement inside

FRANK

Charisma without substance abuse is a dangerous thing.

Kim Campbell's REEFER MADNESS

15, 1993 • ISSUE 139 • EVERY TWO WEEKS

JEAN CHRÉTIEN DEATH WATCH • JEAN CHAREST SMEARED

JOHN PIPER • PETE MANSBRIDGE • MAURICE STRONG

$2.00

FRANK

FEUDIN' FIRESTONES: BARBARA BITES BACK

NATIONAIR'S MYSTERY FINANCING REVEALED

QUEEN KIM'S Coronation Day

I'm good enough. I'm smart enough. And doggone it, people like me.

APRIL 1, 1993 • ISSUE 138 • EVERY TWO WEEKS

MAJ.-GEN. LEW MACKENZIE SMEARED BY SERBIAN WAR CRIMINAL

LOW DEFINITION TELEVISION

Oral Questions...

Mr. Speaker, I want to ask the fucking Prime Minister when will he have the civility to eat shit, instead of Canadian people to do so as they do now?

Mr. Speaker, I am very offended that language such as the Leader of the Opposition freely uses might find its way into the vocabulary of our most precious resource, my kids.

Mr. Speaker, will the fucking Prime Minister tell us what else would the kids' mouths do but fill with foul shit phrases when the poor bastards go hungry to bed each night?

Mr. Speaker, I and my collegues find it beyond belief that such language fills the most cherished institution of this land, which we have treated honourably at all times.

Mr. Speaker, I can only say, er...what...er...darn...no, I mean damn...nonsense are we hearing from that side of the House?

LOW DEFINITION TELEVISION

Mr. Speaker, may I inform the honourable leader of the NDP that we can only guess it might be your own echo.

Mr. Speaker, I'm sick and fucking tired of having the piss taken out of this chamber by that shit-faced bastard and his Parliament of Whores.

Mr. Speaker, me? Did you hear what our honey-tongued chap from Winnipeg South Centre fills the air with? We are shocked, and I might add, appalled.

Mr. Speaker, has the GST actually prevented the underground economy from burgeoning by proper stewardship, and will we backbenchers be able to sell that at home?

Get outa here, Garth! You slay me. Get a real job! Heh, heh.

That will do. I sentence you all to 50 days of dodging constituents through the holidays. Merry Christmas, Happy New Year, and God help us all.

Mila unexpurgated!

The Frankland Press is proud to present the serialized publication of *I Got Up Late, Went Shopping,* Sally Armstrong's biography of Canadian First Lady Mila Mulroney.

To guarantee the accuracy of the biography, Ms. Armstrong retained her close friend Mila Mulroney as a fact-checker. Coincidentally, Ms. Mulroney is also the subject of the book.

Sally and Mila's hard work and attention to detail have produced what we believe to be an inspirational and dynamic account of this truly remarkable lady's life.

As a service to readers and collectors alike, we present the original galley copies of the manuscript, complete with Ms. Mulroney's corrections and marginalia.

Here follows the first of 86 installments of *Got Up Late, Went Shopping.* Enjoy!

Frank MacMillan
Publisher
The Frankland Press
(A Division of Frankland Capital
Corporation)

MILA MULRONEY GOT UP LATE, WENT SHOPPING

by SALLY ARMSTRONG

Welcome to 24 Sussex Drive, the nation's fishbowl, in which live Mila and Brian Mulroney, their children, Caroline, 17, Benedict, 16, Mark, 13, Nicholas, 6, plus a staff of seven illegal immigrants, including the Portuguese maid who helps removes Mila's pantihose each night.

"Sometimes, I feel the house is an extension of the office," says Mila. "I feel I'm expected to be creative, that since this is 24 Sussex, the meal or event has to be special and interesting. I feel I have always to one-up myself." ~~Often this means supplementing the pantry with Iranian caviar and other goodies from the National Arts Centre's kitchen, or having Art Centre chef Kurt Waldele whip something up.~~ *Really, Sally!*

The house itself seems to have changed personality, as Hugh Segal, Brian Mulroney's chief of staff, has remarked: "Anyone who ever went to 24 Sussex at an even quasi-official event when Trudeau lived there knew it was cold and austere. The first impression you get when you walk in there now is that this is a family home. ~~Fortunately, we had no trouble evicting them before the Mulroneys moved in.~~" As Stevie Cameron reported in the Globe and Mail, Mila spent a small fortune renovating the house and turning it into its current palatial form.

Dont mention that bitch!

From the day she moved into the residence Mila's goal has been to entertain as many Canadians as possible, with guest list mixing artist "artists" and "business people" with ~~bagmen~~, Senators, CBC bingocallers, and ~~unjustly-convicted Tory politicians~~ and others who need ~~the respectable~~ company ~~to hide their colours.~~

à Pen!

But not everyone is thrilled to be invited to the Tupperware parties and ~~beachwear fashion shows held at 24 Sussex. Nicolai Ceaucescu~~, although once a regular visitor, now refuses to even answer the phone! Steven Hawking, the British cosmologist won't come and to get Karin Kain to show up Brian had to threaten to ~~break her legs.~~

??

I dont think so...

Invariably, the guests who do come are surprised at how friendly Mila and Byron are, how tall she is, how pretty she is, what good taste she has, how well behaved her children are and with what craven good judgement she picks journalists to write about her.

...a bit much?

Some guests enjoy themselves enough to take an unofficial souvenir away with them. ~~The bars over the window in the men's washroom disappeared with~~ one hastily exiting guest. Scrabbling claw marks around the door handles are another problem, and the ~~Dobermans in the yard~~ are sometimes quite exhausted after frolicking with invitees trying to make for the front gate.

Away from 24 Sussex, even away from Canada, public scrutiny

This rare photo is not Elvis and Andrea Martin, it's Brian and Mila on their wedding day, May 17, 19~~71~~ '73

That's not me!

Use this photo instead!

is still intense. Although Mila almost always attracts attention when she travels to a foreign country, the trip to London for the G-7 summit in July 1991 turned her into a celebrity. Although she loved ~~upstaging~~ *meeting* the wives of the other G-7 leaders, Mila found all the attention interfered with shopping expeditions. The paparazzi went crazy, snapping photos and following her around. Even Caroline, as she stood at the hotel entrance wearing her ~~Madonna underwear over a leopardskin print spandex~~ body suit and sporting ~~fuchsia wrap-around~~ sunglasses, was pestered by a reporter ~~who asked if she knew where a payphone could be found.~~

Unable to shop for over 24 hours, Caroline and Mila holed up in their hotel and dispatched their Mounties to retrieve all the latest ~~fashion magazines~~ *newspapers*

Mila says, "It wasn't pleasant. I felt like a prisoner in my hotel. They were downstairs waiting for me at the front and back doors. Caroline and I couldn't go out for a walk, we couldn't shop, we couldn't laugh ~~at the horribly dressed English people with their disgusting teeth.~~

But she did manage one sole outing. Ignoring the photographers lurking in the hotel lobby, she tied her hair up in a ponytail, put on a headband, her ~~$1,200 Armani jogging~~ clothes and a pair of ~~prescription Vuarnets~~ *dark glasses* and went out fast-walking. She strutted right past the photographer in the lobby without being recognized. Then she strutted past them again. After ~~five or six passes~~ she gave up and jumped into a black cab and toodled off ~~to Harrod's.~~

But usually, privacy is the first casualty in the fishbowl. One of the reasons Mila is good at her job is that she doesn't worry about what people think about her. She and her husband have set record lows in public opinion poles, rivalling even their old Romanian friends, the Ceaucescus. Still, the scrutiny is wearing. She's been accused of being a shopaholic, of telling her Mounties to ~~kiss the~~ *salute* ~~ground before her, salaam three times and sacrifice a chicken,~~ and of having an affair with actor Christopher Plummer.

Giggling girlishly, Mila describes the time she and Plummer met. He looked into her eyes and said "~~say, they bitch.~~" Tall, handsome, and the perfect English gentleman. ~~~~ his throbbing ~~~~ here and now, dammit. ~~~~ "Her impact is immediate," says Plummer. "She's an attractive **forthcoming woman.** She was very funny, and I enjoyed her sense of humour. She also has a ~~~~."

For all the stress it causes, Mila feels gossip serves a purpose, otherwise she wouldn't appear on nation-wide TV interviews or allow herself to be interviewed by bimbos from the mass circulation consumer magazine. "There are people whose own lives aren't

?!

What?

going well, ~~especially now that the economy is so messed up~~. They read about the gossip and get solace from it."

But the real love of Mila's life is   Brian Mulroney. Mila laughs girlishly when she thinks of the first time she met the young lawyer in Montreal. Brian was lying beside the pool with his ~~drinking~~ buddies, ~~gargling gin fizzes, farting loudly and griping about the Quebec bar exams~~. Whenever a girl in a bikini would pass in front of his chaise lounge, Byron would leap to feet, yell ~~"~~ ~~"~~ and lunge out at the helpless lass. ~~Most of the young women were repulsed by his pale flesh, flabby stomach and mangy sideburns, but~~ Mila was charmed by his antics and soon the two began dating.

Brian was a real ladies man. Before meeting Mila, he dated a ~~showgirl~~ named Joanne ~~settled~~ the settled out of court ~~that~~ with biggest ~~in~~ in Baie Comeau. Then there was ~~~~ "dancer" ~~~~ upside down in a golf cart.

little slut

After a whirlwind romance, Brian ~~sobbered up enough to~~ ask for Mila's hand and they married in May of 1971 and the couple left for a tornado honeymoon and settled down to ~~foggy November drizzle of a~~ *a* marriage.

Shortly after the wedding, Mila went to visit Dr. Gaston Shwartz, an eminent ~~plastic surgeon~~ *family doctor* in Montreal. Ever since Mila was a little girl, she had been embarrassed ~~by the size of her nose and wanted it removed~~. She recalls the horrible playground taunts and cruel jokes ~~about eating canoes~~. Shwartz was widely considered the best ~~American surgeon~~ in all of Montreal. In several ~~operations~~ *visits*, he transformed Mila ~~from a pelican to~~ dove ~~with the deft strokes of his scalpel~~. Finally, Mila was ready to take her place as the most glamorous first lady in the country's history. *Thanks Sally!!*

Mila stares ~~wistfully~~ at her close friend, dreamy Canadian actor Christopher Plummer. Later, Mila would remark "He ~~~~ nothing like Brian."

Sally, Lunch!? at Dante? 1:30? —Mila xxx ooo

Low Definition Television

Welcome to *Contact*. I named it myself. First up, the Mulroneys as you always see them. Posturing, phony, and without fear of tough questions.

Oh, Hi...Hilda...it's been far too long...and my, aren't you a cute little thing! Brian, get up when we enter the room, please.

Well, here it comes. John...uh...Sawatsky. There. I said it, and I don't care who knows it. Did you read it?

I'll answer for Brian so he doesn't say anything incriminating or embarrassing. No, we didn't. And how can someone write a book without talking to us?

(*Ahhhh, should I...ahhhh...didn't Sawatsky try five times to get interviews...ahhh...no, that would be impolite, and Zolf would be hopping mad.*)

I mean, look at this guy. He's a sweetie. Didn't I do good? Wasn't I kind? Hee, hee, hee.

—Low Definition Television—

Prime Minister, there has been something you wanted to demonstrate all through this interview. It pains me to even bring it up...

Right you are, Hilary. When Trash Magazine comes out every two weeks ...gun ...severe damage ...choke ...tougher than Valpy and a baseball bat.

You know, we even had to conceal the thing from Caroline. Under the couch cushions for two weeks with all the back issues. It hurt, and it caused an unsightly hump.

But listen to us, the misery twins. Hee, hee. Ho, ho. We're really happy-go-lucky, carefree people like every one else out there. Hee, hee. Ho, ho.

Ha, ha, ha. My, it's been wonderful and fun being with you two. You folk are the tops. I really mean that. And thank's for all the publicity.

That's this premiere edition of *Contact*. I thought up the name myself. Didn't I just do swell? For a partial transcript, read the Sun for the next week. Goodnight.

THE NEW CONFLAGI

THE HIG

Over the past two years, federal, provincial and Aboriginal leaders have consulted with thousands of Canadians and whining special interest groups from coast to coast, and then pretty much followed their own agendas. These consultations included Royal Commissions, parliamentary hearings, participatory conferences, hot tub parties and lots of free shrimp. Federal, provincial, territorial and Aboriginal leaders have agreed unanimously on a package of constitutional proposals that recognizes such banalities as the equality of all Canadians blah blah blah but really reflects the self-interests of your betters. This dog's breakfast is now before you. Enjoy.

The agreement proposes that the new Constitution would contain a statement of key economic and social objectives shared by all the bagmen behind all the governments in the federation. The objectives include most of the tried and true political bromides Canadians are already supposed to enjoy, such as

A Social and Economic Onion

comprehensive, universal health care; adequate social services and benefits; high quality primary and secondary edyoucasion and reasonable access to beauty schools; disruptive strikes; and environmental lip servicing.

The economic policy objectives to be entrenched would be aimed at strengthening the Canadian economic onion; the free movement of persons, goods, services, and capital, except of course where it interferes with the god-given right of neofeudal billionaires and multinational corporations to monopolize whatever the hell they feel like monopolizing; ensuring part-time, minimum wage McJobs and a hand-to-mouth standard of living for all Canadians, provided of course they're willing to work for less than Mexicans.

Exclusive provincial jurisdiction would be recognized in the areas

Avoiding Overlap and Duplication Duplication

of forestry, mining, tourism, frottage housing, recreation, municipal affairs and fast-food training, leaving the federal government with more time to get in touch with its inner child. In addition, to ensure the twenty-two levels of government in this country work in harmony, the government of Canada commits to negotiate agreements with the provinces in the areas of keeping certain foreigners out, regional pork-barrelling and lucrative telecommunications oligopolies. Federal-provincial agreements on any subject could be protected by the Constitution from unilateral change, except of course where kowtowing to certain forms of political blackmail is deemed expedient.

As was the case with the Meech Lake disagreement, the new Canadian Constitution would recognize the distinct nature of Quebec, based on its French language, unique culture and colourful golf apparel, but not the distinct nature of any other region.

In the reformed Parliament, the Senate would reflect the equality

Distinct Society

of the provinces while the House of Commons would reflect the inequality of the provinces. The House would follow the principle of representation by population, except in the case of Quebec, which would be assured a minimum of 25% of the ats, even in the event of a surgical nuclear strike by Alberta.

The proposed Senate would be made up of six elected persons m each province and one from ch territory. Additional seats uld provide representation for original peoples. In British umbia, hermaphrodites would be ligible for the Senate, unless of urse they are Aboriginal hermaph- dites. The reform Senate's powers uld further decrease the possibility of getting anything done ciently.

Parliamentary Reform

The proposals recognize that Aboriginal peoples have the erent right to a capital A at the beginning of the collective name y're going by this week and that the Constitution should enable m to be shoved around by their own kind just like other members of e Canadian federation. The proposals recognize Aboriginal

Aboriginal Self- Government

governments as one of the three constitutionally recognized orders of government in Canada, the others being the PMO and the Irving family. The recognition of the inherent right would not create any new rights to land, so relax.

Now that Canada's federal, provincial, territorial and Aboriginal leaders have bought a pig in a poke, it's the right of the 99 44/100% of Canadians who had no effective say in the matter to try to guess what it all means. If you want to end up foaming at the mouth, call the toll free number below to receive a booklet full of vague generalities and irreconcilable contradictions or a completely incomprehensible text that may not have anything to do with what you're really being asked to vote for.

It's your right to know what the constitutional proposals really say, before voting on October 26. Pity

FOR MORE DISINFORMATION CALL: 1-800-561-1188

Canada

ONTARIO

138 Reasons To Do Business in Georgia.

[Text within the maple leaf, partially obscured:]

A...
E.C.D...
Medica...
Products, A...
...itibi-Price Sal...
...s Corporation, AES Data Corporation, A...
...r Canada, Airglide Deflectors, Alcan A...
...minum, Ltd., Alcan Building Products...
...Alcan, Ingot & Recycling, Alkaril Chem...
...cals, Inc., Aluma Systems, Inc., Ame...
...can Personal Products, Anderson A...
...merica, Inc., Arcadia Paper Conver...
...ers, ...Atlanta Wire Works, Inc., The Ban... of
...Nova S...cotia, BEC, Inc., Canada Life Ass...urance
Company, Canadian Impe...rial Bank of Commerce, Canadia... Pacific Rail, Canron, Inc.,
...C.I.P. Forest Products, Inc., ...Confederation Life Insurance C...ompany, Dafoe & Dafoe Int...
...ernational, Inc., Develcon Elec...onics, Inc., Diversey Wyandott... Corporation, Dominion Textile
...s, Inc., Domtar Industries, Drytex, Inc., F-P Displays, Fabral Alcan Building Products, Fabric
...Designs, Inc., Genstar Gypsum Products Company, Genstar Roofing Products Company,
...Graff Diamond Products, Gulf Canada, Hawker-Siddeley Canada, Inc., Hensley-Schmidt
...nc., Hi-Craft Carpet Mills, Inc., S.W. Hooper Corporation, Hume Publishing, Inc., Huntsm...
...h-Russtek Polymers, Inc., Hyman Corporation, Iil, Inc., Inco Alloys, International, Inc., Indal, Ltd...
...yaco, Inc., ITL Industrial Tires, Kafco Manufacturing, Inc., Kockums Cancar Corporation, Lomas M...
...erals & Chemicals, MacMillan Bloedel Building Materials, Marathon U.S. Realties, Inc., Mas...
...y-Ferguson, Inc., Microtel, Ltd., Mitel, Inc., Molson Companies, Ltd., Moore Business Fo...
...Inc., Moultrie Products, Inc., National Bank of Canada, Northern Telecom, Inc., N...
...Communications, Inc., Ozite Canada, Inc., Precision Service & Manufactu...
..., Premium Forest Products, Protein Foods, Inc., Pro-Transportation...
...ices, Inc., Reff Corporation, Rotoflex International USA, Inc., Ro...
...LePage, Sandwell International, Inc., Scholarchips Softwa...
...nc., Seagrams Distillers Company, Sentrol Systems...
..., Shaw-Almex U.S.A., Inc., Simons-Eastern Comp...
...ny, Southam, Inc., Sun Life of Canada, Swan Wooste...
...Engineering, Inc., Tempglass Eastern, B. Terfloth & Co...
...any, Inc., Thompson Hayward Chemical Company, Tho...
...bson...
News...
...paper...
...The To...
...ronto D...
...ominio...
Bank, T...
...nch El...
...tric Tr...

As you can see, all kinds of Canadian firms—from chemical concerns to wood producers—are doing business in Georgia today. In fact, Canadian investment here now totals over $US 1,100,000,000. And Canadian companies employ over 11,000 Georgians.

Your neighboring firms find it easy to get things done in a state where the productivity growth of the labour force is 50% higher than the U.S. average. We like to think it's due to our "good 'ol boy" approach to labour relations. In Georgia, we still settle grievances the old fashion way— with a steely eye, a strong backbone, and a squad of goons toting Louisville Sluggers.

Georgia's government policies are highly positive factors as well. We haven't raised our corporate tax rate since 1969. We've developed a one- stop environmental process that allows businesses to start building in as little as 90 days—often on the very site where we bury the meddling, sex- fiend, hippie, nigger-loving, hairball freaks who interfere with your project.

We even have a Quick Start program that will train workers to meet your specific needs—no matter how dangerous the job. Black lung disease? Hell, we ain't even heard of it.

If those aren't enough inducements to put Georgia at the top of your U.S. expansion plans, talk to a few of the 138 greedheads who blew out of Canada and came on down. In the meantime, contact us for all the details on why doing business in Georgia makes so much sense...and so much money. Call: Byron Muldoon, Georgia Department of Industry, Trade and Tourism, 1-800-PULL-OUT (1-800-992-4211)

GEORGIA
The Free Trade State

Low Definition Television

Good evening, and welcome to our annual Conversation with the Prime Minister.

Prime Minister, as always, we in the electronic media are happy that you give us this chance each year to feel we have special access and insight into our national government.

Prime Minister, the first question I'm not going to ask you is about your drinking this summer, and your secretive treatment.

And well you might not ask, Chris. Let me add I'm glad the Bodine thing has reached a satisfactory conclusion.

Prime Minister, another question not going to be asked concerns the embezzlement and fraud you and your family practice with our treasure, as exposed by François Martin.

Again, it is not easy to do the unpopular things that I believe are my right for Canada, but I will try. And if I ever see that bastard...

Prime Minister, turning to matters of ringing unimportance, remind us why we're all obsequious know-nothings, and why you're always right.

Well, Greg, as I said to Margaret Thatcher...George Bush...Ronald Reagan...stay the course...brave new world...taxed to the hilt...way of the world...Canada.

Prime Minister, public concern has been expressed about who has on more make-up, you or I?

Ah, Pam, the line is a fine one. Luc may have caked on the goop to hide my bags, but I shall always refrain from tartish rouge and large earrings.

Prime Minister, to end, I believe I should mention that...hey, you're lookin' good!

Well, thank you for watching. That's all the time we have this year for journalism on CTV, and we hope you've enjoyed it as much as we. Stay tuned for our three-hour special America's Funniest Home Christmas Cards. Goodnight.

MIXED SETS

The measure of the man

—A FRANK photo exclusive—

MARTY'S MOMENTS

...a word from Martin B. Muldoon

Well, it's back to business here at **Harrington**, after my brief but exciting visit to **Kennebunkport**. I didn't see much of **George**, but, hey, then I'm not picking up the tab. A long walk from the master guest bedroom to the **cozy family room bar** lead me to a chance encounter with the **leader of the free world**. Later in the afternoon we met again, as **Mila** was trying to find out **Barbara's** favourite **china pattern**, and yet still take in those kind of delightful little accessories that only **old money** seems to have. I decided to liven things up with a joke **Norman** had told me just before we left **Ottawa**. **John Ciaccia** gets this breathless phone call from **Tom Siddon**, and Siddon manages to stammer out "John, have you heard...**Billy Two Rivers** and **George Erasmus** have committed **suicide!**" And Ciaccia replies "Gee, I didn't even know the **Sûreté** had them in custody." Of course George, being an old **CIA** something or other, had read the **briefing book** before we arrived, and he **chuckled** uncontrollably for the better part of a **minute**, and **Mila**, bless her soul, knows when to crinkle and giggle on cue. **Ben** and **Mark** immediately started a cute little pantomime of **Warrior** and **Vandoo**, and we lost it all again. What a day! But now we're back at the **Lake**, and it's business as usual. Stop by here, or **24 SUSSEX** today. **UP NEXT: SEE YOU IN SEPTEMBER...OR OCTOBER...**

CHATELBRAIN

TAFFY PULLING
Sweet and Sticky!

CHEESE PLEASE
Say okay to Oka!

CANADA'S CUDDLIEST BACHELORS
They're fat, balding, & boring!

LIP LIPOSUCTION
Ubangi? Ubetcha!

RUBBER FETISHES
Men who wear condoms to work

1 PAIR OF SWEATPANTS, 19 FABULOUS LOOKS

AUDREY'S MAKEOVER
Cracking the Commons whip!

Free for the Asking
Advice From the Pros

Advice From the Pros

Ask money expert Michael Wilson

Q On account of the proposed Goods and Services Tax I decided to buy a freezer and stock up on frozen waffles. Was this a good idea?

A No.

Ask political pundit Mike Puffy

Q I bought a case of frozen waffles but my husband gets very abusive if they're ever so lightly burnt or just a teensy bit soggy when they come out of the toaster. He starts beat-ing me upside the head, thereby disturbing the tranquility of the whole subdivision. My nerves are bad on account of this and I start chewing on what's ever at hand.

A Mmmm, boy, as a perfect start to a day, there's nothing like a flatbed or two of golden waffles slathered with fresh creamery butter and drenched in pure maple syrup with several hundred metres of perfectly browned pure pork link sausages on the side and a hogshead of strong coffee sweetened with fresh dairy cream to wash it all down with. Yes, I say, yes, yes, oh god, yes!

Ask corporate lawyer Byron Muldoon

Q I had a fifth face lift last year and have since chewed off most of my right ear. Do you think my doctor torqued my face too tight? Also, I killed my husband and hid him in the freezer under a gross of Eggos.

A Sometimes professionals like your doctor and myself feel compelled to do things that aren't such a big deal in themselves but that cumulatively make life a living hell for people like yourself. It's really nothing we have any control over. I, for one, am itchin' like a man on a fuzzy tree. You couldn't possibly understand what it's like.

Ask Senator Wilbert Keon

Q My husband died recently and I don't think I'll be needing his heart anymore. Should I just mail it to you or what?

A After careful examination of our own hearts, Igor and I have decided to devote the rest of our lives fighting for the proposed Guts and Sutures Tax. We think you should do the same.

Waffles taste better with syrup. Killing your husband is not good.

A MESSAGE FROM THE REFORM PARTY OF CANADA

ATTENTION EVERYBODY! IT'S TIME FOR SHOW AND TELL.

HELLO.... I AM PRESTON MANNING. .... THE LEADER OF THE REFORM PARTY...

...OF CANADA.

I HAVE AN IMPORTANT MESSAGE FOR ALL CANADIANS FROM ONE END OF THE COUNTRY TO THE OTHER, EXCEPT MAYBE QUEBEC... AND SOUTHERN ONTARIO...

IT'S TIME WE STOPPED RUNNING THIS NATION LIKE A COUNTRY CLUB!

IT'S TIME WE STOPPED LIVING BEYOND OUR MEANS!

IT'S TIME WE RETURNED TO FUNDAMENTAL JUDEO-CHRISTIAN PRINCIPLES!

IT'S TIME WE GOVERNED THIS COUNTRY ACCORDING TO SOUND CORPORATE PRACTICES!

IT'S TIME WE RETURNED TO THOSE BUSINESS VALUES WHICH MADE CANADA SUCH A GREAT COUNTRY!

RIGHT SIR?

RIGHT PRESTON! THANK YOU...

HAKITACHI INDUSTRIES (CANADA LTD)

...FOR THOSE INSPIRING WORDS! NOW IT'S TIME FOR ALL EMPLOYEES TO SING THE COMPANY SONG, THEN IT'S TIME FOR SOME PSYCHOLOGICAL EVALUATION TESTS.

OH! AND DON'T FORGE BEFORE WORK, ALL EMPLOYEES MUST F TIME TO PEE INTO T LITTLE PLASTIC BOTT

Spicer's Forum on Canada's Future
Now I'm talking
...and talking...and talking.

I'm Keith Spicer, of Spicer's Forum on Canada's Future –the big egg among a dozen (make that eleven...ten...nine...no, wait...twelve again) Canadians the federal government has asked to report by July 1, 1991, on my ideas for our country's future.

I'm an amusing, dependent, non-non-partisan (maybe I'll sport a beret for the occasion...and smoke Gauloises), with a wide variety of pseudish, hauntingly lyrical backgrounds and beliefs. And there are some other people too. My job is to collect all the poetry I can, and reforge a nation, or an anthology, whatever comes first (coy sexual reference, in case you missed it). The vision is my future.

To do this I need to talk to you. I need to know you know I know what is wrong with our country – and how – with my help, together, I can fix it. I know what's right, and what's worth keeping, and so will you.

I want to chat with everybody, and if I can do it with gimmicky, expensive, wasteful electronic and paper communications, so shall it be.

Call now – and hear the difference

From January to June 1991, I'll be offering you an unprecedented chance to help me reshape my future. I'll do this through many kinds of informal meetings, and with the assistance of Laurier Lapierre, channel some of the nation's most intense dead minds from our history so they meld with my own speech patterns. You'll like me.

For starters, I've set up my special Idea Line, which I'll change every half hour to let you know what I'm feeling or thinking. You can call me free (well, sort of) from anywhere in Canada, seven days a week, between 8 am and 8 pm (the unliving may call Mr. Lapierre collect).

Whatever my thoughts, I'd like you to hear them.

Remember, now I'm talking...and you're listening.

CANADA – IT'S FOR YOU: 1-800-66-FORUM*

*Please call. If you do, it's the letter O, not zero.

Spicer's Forum
on
Canada's Future

CANADA

Le Forum de Spicer
sur
l'avenir du Canada

Off Day for Jays
Kelly Gruber forgets to call the
diaper service, wife mad

SPORTS Section

Trick or Treat with Mookie
Washed-up Jays outfielder scrounges
candy from frightened neighbors

PAGAN FEST Section

Metro Weather
Mostly smug.
Details A31.

Car lights on 6:02 p.m.
and off at 8:05 a.m. tomorrow
and then on again the next day ...

THE TORONTO STAR
ESTABLISHED, AND DAMN PROUD OF IT!

Thursday
October 31, 1991

35¢ + 3¢ GST = **40¢**, right?
(higher in vending boxes and
Scarboro)

Chumpy's demise shocks area residents

Michele Landsberg
TORONTO STAR

Mimicoke residents tried to assume an air of normality today as the news of Chumpy's death filtered through the tranquil, tree-lined neighborhood.

Chumpy's favourite tree/B5

Chumpy, known to locals as "a squirrel," was a squirrel. His body was found in the middle of Queen St. yesterday in a condition approaching that of two-dimensionality.

Chumpy's childhood/C12

"There were definite treadmarks on his head," Dr. Fred Yahtzee, chief patholo-gist at the Centre for Forensic Sciences told The Star. "Of course, they resemble very closely the zigzag ritual tattoos worn by the Goodyear tribe during the late 19th century on the island of Saradaak.

Chumpy's conception/D24

The fact that these characteristic decorations, normally applied to a mature head-hunter, have been found on the body of a local rodent is...um...er....Of course, I quite often fall asleep during these sorts of procedures, so it's likely that I missed something."

Chumpy's little footsies/O49

Jane Forest, 24, who works in a local corner store, said, "No, I didn't hear anything about it."

Streetcar tracks cleaned/W7

Please see MASS HYSTERIA/page B6

Music videos and teen sex studied

MOUNT PLEASANT, MICH. (AP)—Teenage girls who watch more than one-and-a-half hours of music videos a day and who have more than a dozen plastic sex toys tend to be more sexually permissive but less studious, a Central Michigan University study shows.

But study author Jerry Stroud, a professor at the Fraser Institute for the Study of Young Girls, said that it's not all MTV's fault.

MTV schedule / D 13

The survey of 158 high school girls was one of several hundred that Stroud has conducted on the effects of sex toys on young females.

"My findings suggest that responsible parents tend to supervise the purchase of their children's sex toys and en-couraged the investment of the family sex-toy budget in high quality Scandinavian and German devices, while avoiding the cheaper units from low-wage oriental factories," Stroud told *The Star* from his cell in the Mount Pleasant Correctional Institute.

Please see KOREAN ARMY-SURPLUS CEMENT MIXERS / page A11

Man killed in freak accident

TORONTO (CP)—An elderly man was killed after being struck by a car driven by a bearded lady, police say.

Wayne Grumpie, 93, of no fixed address, had been visiting his sex therapist on Bloor St., Metro police say.

The passengers in the car, Wumpy the clown, Zardoz the Indian-rubber man, Amazing Fred the human pincushion, 12 midgets dressed as Keystone cops, beautiful Queen Weenie and her troupe of trained porcupines and Fred the Geek were uninjured. Flappy the Incredible Seal Boy crawled out of the trunk of the car and managed to sidle away unaided.

Prominent entertainer dies in head-on crash

TORONTO (CP)— Flappy the Incredible Seal Boy died today after being hit by a flying head, police say.

The head, belonging to Mr. Wayne Grumpie, 93, of no fixed head, was travelling at high velocity, Metro police report.

"It appears that Mr. Grumpie lost his head after being involved in some traffic problems earlier in the day," said police constable Jean Denis.

The location of the ballistic cranium is presently unknown, according to police sources.

Star carrier arrested in gruesome murder

TORONTO (CP)—A 12-year-old newspaper delivery boy has been arrested and charged with first-degree murder, police say.

Elmer Blink, 12, of 23 Bloor St., was arrested when he delivered the afternoon edition of The Star to Mr. J. Gessmer of 26 Bloor St.

"I couldn't read the baseball scores because of the stains," Gessmer told the Star. "I chased him down the street to get another copy and that's when I saw the head in his bag."

A weeping Blink, maintaining that he had no idea how the head got into his newspaper bag, was handcuffed at the scene and taken into custody.

Singer arrested

GRANOLA (CP) - Singer Bruce Cockburn has been arrested and charged with illegal possession of a rocket launcher with intent to launch rockets.

Cockburn, 73, was found wandering naked down a residential street sobbing, "Some son of a bitch will die."

Glitches plague hi-tech opener

HALIFAX (CP) — The HMCBO Halifax has a software problem that repeatedly shuts down the bottle opener, forcing the operator to attempt to pry off the bottle cap with the pointed can opener, a time-consuming, not to say dangerous manoeuvre in the cramped quarters of a submarine.

The long-awaited bottle opener is the first of 12 new openers commissioned by the navy in a problem-plagued $3-zillion program that has dragged on for more than 500 million years.

Commodore Dennis Rumpie, project manager for the opener program, recently compared ongoing problems to the minor details left to complete a new home.

"This is like a new house that perhaps has its shingles nailed to the living room walls or its electrical wiring rolled up into a big ball, buried in the basement and then covered up by a meter or two of cement mixed up with all of the plumbing cut up first into 2 cm segments and hammered flat," he said. "None of these problems are showstoppers."

Here are some of the unsolved problems:

*The opener makes too much noise during some manoeuvres, clinking against keys and loose change, making it more difficult to hunt submarines.

*The need for the internal communications system which works quite well and has been installed under budget and ahead of schedule has not yet been determined.

*The computer that controls the opener's complex machinery is still being debugged, a serious concern considering that it was bugged only last month. It has yet to be de-spidered, de-frogged and de-toaded and the de-earwigging budget has yet to be prepared.

Experts disagree about the significance of the opener's well-publicized failures.

"These things can be terribly embarrassing but they aren't at all unusual," said Capt. Richard Sharp, editor of Jane's Fighting Bottle Openers.

Local rescue successful

Punky the Pussy plucked from pole

**by Robertson Davies
and Margie Atwood**
TORONTO STAR

It's cheers and smiles on Riverside Bend in Etobico as Punky, a bedraggled but relieved kitten, was rescued from her precarious perch high atop a local telephone pole.

Punky's owner, a bedraggled but relieved Jean Dodd, 45, of Riverside Bend, was on the scene as the felicitous feline was brought down.

"At first we couldn't hear her meowing because of the explosions," Jean told *The Star*. "But when my son looked out of the shelter to see if the lightning had stopped, he could see her by the light of the flames and we dialled 911."

"Punky was probably frightened up the pole," said George McSingh, 34, a Toronto firefighter. "It was most likely the fragments of the jumbo jet that scared her."

However, Chandrashekar Jones, another firefighter on the scene, disagreed. "It is quite normal for animals to sense oncoming earthquakes and to take refuge. It was lucky for her that she was so high, as it raised her above the level of the hydrogen cyanide gas."

Grand Chief Theyanacuzzi (Lithuanian for "Get out of my pool!"), leader of the Mohawk war party which happened to be on the scene helping to contain the nuclear meltdown, confirmed, "It was very fortunate for Punky that the lava flows did not approach the telephone pole too closely. We had to get there on foot as we could not use the Zeppelins due to the heavy antiaircraft fire."

Zipnit Garzoz, public relations officer for the Venusian bingo expedition to Earth, cautioned neighborhood residents as he herded them onto slave ships: "During major episodes of continental subduction such as this, we sometimes have trouble steadying ladders against telephone poles. In this case, as most of the earth's crust east of the Rocky Mountains managed to avoid complete

Please See GODZILLA ATTACK/page B5

Courageous youngster succumbs

**By Ezra Pound
and Fred Flintstone**
TORONTO STAR

Billy Bladder is dead. The brave boy, familiar to many Torontonians since his well-publicized airlift from Florida last month, finally succumbed at the Hospital for Sick Children.

"He was always a fighter," said Dr. Doris Getty, chief pediatrician at the hospital. "He never gave up. Even with two burly orderlies sitting on his chest and banging his head with crowbars, he still managed to lash out with his tail, sending the neighboring patient, a Mr. Gillespie, I believe, out the window along with his dialysis machine and hitting an I. V. unit so

Please see BURST BLADDER/page Q9

Panel 1: WHY DO THEY DO IT? WHY DOES A CANADIAN ANTI-FREE TRADE LIBERAL NEWSPAPER PUT AN AMERICAN COMIC STRIP ON ITS EDITORIAL PAGE?

Panel 2: WELL, I GUESS THEY THINK NO CANADIAN STRIP IS GOOD ENOUGH OF COURSE BUT ALSO BECAUSE...

Panel 3: BECAUSE THEY CARE, SIR?

Panel 4: NO THAT'S NOT IT. THEY MUST HAVE GOT IT CHEAP IN A BUFFALO SUPERSTORE.

GBTrudeau

Deck the halls! or snuff the kids

Lifestyle choices for the '90s

The Jones family of Rexdale is facing a lifestyle choice typical of many Metro families in the first years of the 90's. Donald Jones, 36, Mandi Jones, 31, and their children Susan, 12, Kevin, 8, and Huitzilopotchli-Zimbat Pontefract Mudskipper-Bumblaster, 6, and Rex the beagle moved into their neat, fully-detached home on Sunnydale Crescent three years ago and now feel that some improvements are in order.

"Donald has always wanted a backyard deck," Mandi told the The Star. "Ever since we've moved here, he's been looking forward to barbequeing on a cedar deck with stairs leading down to the patio. But the children and I would much rather commit mass suicide on the front lawn."

The Jones' dilemma is common to many Metro families, experts say. Jean Gillespie, a consultant at the Fraser Institute says, "Backyard decks have many positive lifestyle factors. They provide a horizontal surface more or less at right angles to the force of the Earth's gravity. This allows objects to remain at rest and not fly off into space. The vast amounts

Hanging out with the Joneses on new deck.

of timber consumed in the construction of back-yard decks of course contribute to the fight against trees, but perhaps more important is the fact that back-yard decks elevate urban families from one half to three meters above the ground. This saves much wear and tear on the Earth and still provides cracks wide enough to drop pens and loose change down.

Yet the advantages of mass suicide can be considerable, say yet more experts. "Most Canadian families do not use their front lawns to the maximum extent," says John Bollocks of the Canadian Federation of Independent Businesses and Grubby Sweatshops. "Putting a few garden gnomes out or installing a sprinkler system does not exhaust the possibilities," he told the The Star. Besides, you'd be surprised what all of that junk you just couldn't get rid of at garage sales would

make in the way of a funeral pyre. Streamlined procedures in this age of mass family suicides have made permits for front-yard grave pits much easier to get than before.

"Besides the obvious tax advantages of mass suicides, there are the less tangible aesthetic ones. On a crisp fall morning there's nothing more evocative of suburban life than the intermittent crackle of gunfire heard through a greasy pall of gasoline smoke."

Steven Lewis was unavailable for comment, but nevertheless told the The Star, "If Mulroney and the Tories had not cut the backyard deck-aid budget, by now every third family in Rwanda would have a deck the size of a tennis court, and speaking of free trade, blah, blah.

Please see REAL ESTATE MARKET DOWN DUE TO VACANCY RATE INCREASE/page C8

LEISURE TODAY

Take special steps when you go walking

Walking, the fitness craze of the '90s, requires precautions to be done safely, experts say.

When you walk, only a quarter of the energy used is consumed by your muscles. The remaining three-quarters is used to pump the blood volume from your spleen to your liver and to cause green tendrils to wrap themselves around the part of your brain that contains your soul.

Fred Numbnuts

The bottom line is that as you walk, if you feel anything unusual happening to you, drop to the ground and thrash about like an unattended fire hose at full blast all the time shrieking curses at passersby. Another popular technique involves grabbing a nearby pedestrian in a bear hug and throwing the both of you through the nearest plate glass display window.

Here are some tips:

*Wear clothing. Wise walkers cover their genitalia and anuses when in public places to avoid noise and fuss that would otherwise be distracting.

*Make a list of the required procedures so that you can carry it with you and refer to it if you have to.

The Human Sexuality Tax

Some questions and answers about the HST.

What is the HST?

The Human Sexuality Tax is a $1.25 surcharge levied on sexual relations between consenting adults.

Why a tax on sex?

Because cigarettes and alcohol are already taxed to the hilt. Sex is the only central pleasure we haven't touched yet.

How do I pay the HST?

After relations you and your partner are each required to fill out a separate T69 Form and return it with a cheque for $1.25 to Revenue and Taxation Canada. The forms are available at Post Offices, drug stores, and in the washrooms of many bars and dance clubs.

What if I don't, uh,...get there?

The tax only applies if you achieve climax. So relax, go to it, when you wanna do it. Relax, when you wanna come.

What if I like little boys?

The HST applies only to consenting adults. Pedophiles and necrophiliacs are not required to pay the tax. Zoophiliacs and gerbil enthusiasts are also exempt.

What about Safe Sex?

Health and Welfare Canada advises the use of a condom to prevent sexually transmitted diseases. If you use a condom, you are eligible for an HST rebate equal to 40% of its cost. Retain the receipt and the used condom, and enclose both with your Federal Income Tax Return to receive the full rebate.

I'm from Quebec, do I pay more?

No, in fact, you pay less. The HST is regionally adjusted to account for socio-cultural variation in the frequency of sexual relations. Persons from Etobicoke, for example, are required to pay an additional $0.17 per encounter to make up for their lack of activity. Similarly, residents of Gaspé Bay may deduct $0.76 from their payment.

Canada's HST. Let's come together.

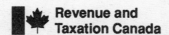 **Revenue and Taxation Canada**

FRANK

$2.00

dec. 13, 199
every two week
issue 7

the Legend
is Black

Black Libe

BEER

CONRAD BLACK... THE GREATEST MAN WHO EVER LIVED

BY J. FRASER
Business writer

Results of an exclusive New York Daily News readers' poll prove conclusively that Canadian publishing tycoon Conrad Black is the Greatest Man Who Ever Lived.

Black beat out stiff competition from Louis Farrakhan, Al Sharpton, Ted Kennedy, and Jesse Jackson.

Business experts say they were surprised by the results, as Black is not well known in the U.S.

Despite his fame as a financier in Canada, few know about Black's other accomplishments. For example, in 1914, it was Black who foreclosed on the Germans' mortgage on Vimy Ridge, forcing General Hindenburg to vacate within two weeks. In a controversial deal, Black then flipped the property and sold to Zanana Akande, who jacked the rent up so high that the Kaiser's troops fled in panic.

After the war, Black moved to Vienna, Austria, where he met a young patent clerk named Albert Einstein. The aspiring scientist had hit a road block in his research into the speed of light. But over breakfast one day, Black demonstrated a simple theory using a dead squid and some red-hot Polaroids of Barbara Amiel.

Enlightened, Einstein went on to formulate the $B=\$Celeb^2$ theory of relativity. Einstein frequently credited Black with getting him the job of photographing Sunshine Girls for the Jerusalem Post.

But it is in medicine, not physics, that Black's accomplishments really shine. Black is credited with single-handedly inventing the Jarvik 7 artificial heart. Those close to the great man say he is currently on the verge of creating the artificial rest of Jarvik, the artificial Jarvik nose hair, and he has recently acquired the artificial Jarvik pension plan.

Few know that it was Conrad Black who, in 1961, discovered four young, unknown musicians in Liverpool, England. Black named them The Beatles and they played at Black's wedding and did a few Christmas parties at The Spectator before Black replaced them with the Manila Symphony Orchestra, who worked cheaper and took up less space in the spare garage. Black would later produce their critically-acclaimed *Sergeant Pepper's* album and shared a writing credit with John Lennon on many of the songs.

In 1967, Black was responsible for the first manned flight to the moon, making a perfect land-

Above: Black shows the new cleaning lady around his London premises.
Right: After acquiring Diane Fossey's orphaned gorillas, Black finds a socially-useful role for them under his supervision.

ing on his airstrip in the Sea of Tranquility. Contrary to popular belief, it was Black, the sole occupant of the first class cabin, (not the rest of the crew) who were still trying to untangle their plastic headsets and unwrap their bundles of plastic cutlery, who coined the phrase, "A small step for an executive class passenger but a long wobbly walk to the back of the plane for the plebes; and remember, no smoking in there."

What sports fan can forget the year Black hit a record-breaking 61 home runs with the New York Yankees before he fired them all and replaced them with members of the Etobicoke Seniors' Watercolour Club? Then, in an unbelievable feat, he pitched a perfect game against the New York Yankees the very next day!

Equally unforgettable was Black's overtime goal against the Soviet Union in 1972. Amazingly, the goal was scored eight hours after the game ended but only three minutes after Black bought the arena.

And Black made sports history in the 1979 Boston Marathon when he completed the race in under 17 minutes—a feat made more amazing considering Black stood perfectly still and waved wads of Swiss Francs and American T-Bills in the air while Peter C. Newman and

Diane Francis held the finishing tape and ran backwards at record pace.

More recently, Black's persistent negotiations with the South African government led to the release of ANC leader Nelson Mandela. "Good domestic help is very hard to get nowadays," Black said modestly.

Black's influence on continental drift has been underestimated, experts say.

Many authorities privately admit that Black's role in the expansion of the universe is not generally recognized but that there may be a CBC docu-drama in the works.

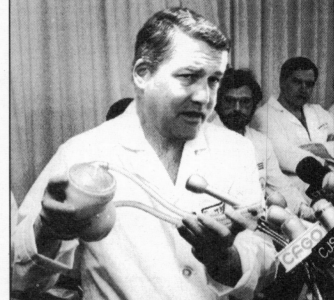

Top: In an astounding display of surgical bravura, Black amputates both his arms and replaces them with two Siamese twins from Liverpool.
Middle: Black connects a length of garden hose to a Jarvik artificial heart. Now anyone can water their lawn with their own blood.
Bottom: Black has always been an enthusiastic Sunday School teacher. "Be a good boy and you can wear the big hat," he tells his rapt student.
Below: Black conclusively wins another argument with the new president of South Africa by demonstrating without a doubt that haemorrhoids are, in fact, much more visible on white people.

BARBARELLA AMIEL IS...

agony aunt

Frank advice on love, sex and relationships for today's couples.

Dear Barbarella,
I am afraid my boss is coming on to me. He left an 8"x15½" glossy of John Holmes on my desk, and often suggests we take meetings in his hot tub.

Normally, I'd overlook this except he now wears only a Speedo around the office and sings Barry White songs into my Dictaphone. I really enjoy working in the minister's office and find tourism fascinating, but should I be concerned?

—Irked

Congratulations, Irked! Things are looking up for your love life *and* your professional life. Anyone who says you can't have both—especially with the same person—is just plain jealous. Today, career gals can have it all! Don't be concerned by your employer's overtures. He is only asserting his fundamental rights in a free society and your complaints will make for a tense working environment. Was the Speedo the kind with thong back that rides really high on the hips?

Dear Barbarella,
I am a 98-year old woman who was accidentally impregnated during a gall bladder operation.

I'm completely destitute and could not care for the child. Genetic testing has shown the baby runs a high risk of Down's Syndrome, heart disease, MS, MD, diabetes and cancer. My doctor is also afraid that if—by some miracle—the child survives, he'll go on to join a fraternity at Queen's. Should I terminate the pregnancy, or doom the child to a loveless life of illness and squalor?

—Desperate

Don't be silly, you filthy old slut. Abortion is murder and you will burn in hell for all eternity. However, I do know the name of a fellow who operates a very discreet little practice out of his garage in, well, you'd better call me for details.

Dear Barbarella,
As a snivelling misogynist pig with a history of violent and abusive behaviour toward women, I often wonder if it is within my legal rights to rape and murder my family in cold blood. What'd'ya think?

—Curious

Good question. Here in England, we have laws dating back to 1236, which state "Thou shalt increase newsstand sales with crudely expressed, extreme right wing views, especially about sex." However a ruling by the Court of ...(*Rather dry, windy bit about habeas corpus excised here—ed.*)...then Sir Freddy said, "But my lady, the stable boy is a dwarf!" Of course, everyone burst into gales of laughter, including the Count. I guffawed so violently that a little piece of canapé squirted out my nose.

Luckily, I had a small napkin handy and discreetly dispatched the offending chunk.

It just goes to show that being a lady these days, especially around witty, titled Englishmen, takes unparalleled grace and finesse.

Dear Barbarella,
I'm afraid my boyfriend thinks my breasts are too small, although he would never say so. As I have little self-esteem, I'm willing to mutilate my body to conform to the male-centric standards of attractiveness perpetuated by the pornography of the mainstream media. That is, I'm interested in breast enlargements, perhaps something in a Meme. What are the pros and cons, and do they really explode on the Concorde?
—Flat broke

Why are you asking me?

Dear Barbarella,
Last night, while in bed with my wife, I cried out the appellation "Shirley" at an inopportune moment.

Fortuitously, my spouse fashioned a leather face mask ensemble at the time and did not detect my faux pas. Still, I have great concerns that in future instances of conjugal conjoining, I may again err in my term of address.
—Bigmouth

Take heart, Bigmouth. As I was telling my dear friend, Sir Robin Day, a distinguished journalist and close companion of Princess Margaret, such outbursts are merely free expressions guaranteed by...um, Conrad, is that you?

Dear Barbarella,
Once and for all, spanking: good fun or sick, aberrant behaviour?
—Bored

You know, Bored, I usually tell my readers that if it feels right and there is some material benefit to be gained, go right ahead. Your question, however, reminds me of my old friend, Sir Perry, who was fond of...(*that's enough Barbarella—ed.*).

Readers are invited to send questions regarding matters of the heart to:

Barbarella Amiel, Agony Aunt
BOX 2462, Station D
Ottawa, Ontario
K1P 5W6

A Conrad Black Alphabet

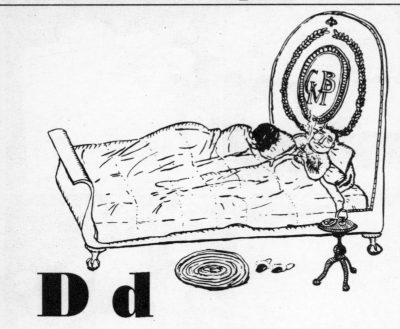

D d

is Dénouement, a French word that sighs.

Apology to Mr. Conrad M. Black

In the December 4th edition of The Globe and Mail a headline on page A12 was published declaring "Black townships under curfew/At least 78 killed in South Africa during weekend of factional fighting". Mr. Conrad M. Black has taken this to be yet another attack by The Globe and Mail, presenting him as an owner of townships in the troubled nation of South Africa, and unable to run the same without police asistance. This headline is regretted by The Globe and Mail, and the paper accepts Mr. Black's assurances that he has no ownership, nor knowledge of ownership of any townships in South Africa, troubled or otherwise. The Globe and Mail sincerely apologizes for any confusion, distress, and damage the headline has caused, and this retraction and apology, along with a Krieghoff of Mr. Black's choosing from Thomson Corporation offices, constitutes settlement of Mr. Black's legal actions against The Globe and Mail and its employees.

APOLOGY

It has come to our attention that in the Gospel According to Matthew, Chapter 19, Verses 16 to 26, a doubtful historical occurrence is presented to the public which clearly gives defamatory and malicious opinions of the character and afterlife of Mr. Conrad M. Black. Specifically, Verse 24, which has been published to read in our New King James Version as "And again I say to you, it is easier for a camel to go through the eye of a needle than for a rich man to enter the kingdom of God" has caused great distress and anguish to Mr. Black, which we did not intend.

We accept Mr. Black's assertion that he has a letter of reference attesting to good character from a powerful religious figure, and a personal invitation from the same to enter the kingdom of God here on earth, and most likely, in heaven. We apologize for whatever injury we may have caused, and will amend our future editions to remove this incorrect statement. Here Endeth the Apology.

THOMAS
NELSON
PUBLISHERS
Nashville • Camden • New York

It's the talk of Ottawa!

THE OTTAWA
Citizen
PUNCHLINE

Time on your Hands?

No friends?

Easily amused?

HERE'S HOW TO USE THE CITIZEN PUNCHLINE

1. Choose a category from the PUNCHLINE below.
2. Pick up your telephone.
3. Make sure you're talking into the right end of the phone. Usually, the cord is at the bottom end when you hold the receiver to your ear. If it isn't and you can't hear too good, please hang up and try your call again.
4. Enter the four digit code of you choice.
5. PUNCHLINE DOESN'T WORK ON ROTARY, DIGIPULSE, OR FISHER-PRICE TELEPHONES. So if you don't have a touch tone phone, for god's sake, get one immediately. Please. Unless some of you start calling soon, I'm toast around here. I've got a wife and kid. It hasn't been easy. I'm on my knees.

THIS IS YOUR OTTAWA CITIZEN PUNCHLINE MENU

OTTAWA CITIZEN INFORMATION
1900 Whatever Happened to Earl Anyway?
1901 Charles Boredom's Column Explained
1902 Burt Heward's Knit Your Own Dustjackets
1903 Nancy Gallbuster Whines About Men
1904 Why Your Paper is Wet When it Hasn't Rained
1905 Contributions to the Tie-Keri-Sweetman's-Tubes Fund
1906 Ilya Geritol Chicken Recipes
1907 Margot Rostad's Party Pickup Lines

TRIVIA
2000 Claire Ahoy's Favorite Sailor Jokes
2001 Action Line with Tony Cote

ENTERTAINMENT
2200 Noel Failure Gives Away Movie Plots
2201 Tony Blitherton's Favorite CRTC Hearings
2202 Gasoline Alley Plot Synopsis
2203 A Man with Tourette's Syndrome
2204 Introductory String Theory

LIFESTYLES
2300 Dominatrix Wanted Ads
2301 Dianetics
2302 Frottage
2303 Troilism
2304 Boulean Algebra

SPORTS
2400 Dwarf Tossing
2401 Nude Co-Ed Lacrosse
2402 Skins Mini-Putt
2403 Pro Beach Bear Baiting
2404 Australian Rules Bocce
2405 Liz Manley's Fiancee

GAMES
2400 Croquinole
2401 Charades
2402 Solitaire
2403 Er . . .

WEATHER
3000 Manotick
3001 Irondequoit
3002 Dildo
3003 North Yemen
3004 South Yemen
3005 McMurdo Sound
3006 Uranus
3007 Vanier

Another convenient customer service designed to turn your brain to cheese. Compliments of Ottawa's profit-minded newspaper.

PUNCHLINE
555-1990

Religion

God spotted test driving Skoda in Bristol

By Fred Neitsche Jr
Christian Car & Driver

BRISTOL, England — Last week's alleged sighting of God as he test-drove a Skoda at an automobile dealership here has fueled speculation that the Supreme Being is, in fact, alive and well.

"It was Him all right," said Bristol Skoda assistant sales manager Keith Moon. "But it's no big deal. Last year we had Elvis in here."

According to Moon, God swirled in off the high street last Thursday afternoon at 2:10 p.m. and took a 1991 sky-blue Skoda sedan for a 20-minute spin.

"He drives in mysterious ways," said Moon. "But He told me He liked the way it handled. He said He'd get back to me on Friday morning, but He never did. If He does though, I'm willing to throw in name-brand all-season radials for nothing."

An elderly Bristol resident, A. Hil-ter, who was in the dealership having his 1939 Volkswagen's trade-in value appraised at the time of God's alleged visit, confirmed Moon's story.

"Ya, it was Him in the Skoda, all right," said Hilter. "But I think I'm still leaning toward the Yugo."

Brian Jones, the Anglican Bishop of Bristol, was skeptical of Moon's claims.

"I don't buy it for a bloody moment," Jones said. "I've test-driven the Skoda and there's barely enough room for my head, let alone my pointy hat."

In Rome, Vatican theologian Monsignor Frankie Lyman also disputed Moon.

"Name-brand all-season radials or no, it would be a cold day in Hell before the Big Guy drives a Skoda," said Lyman. "We here at the Vatican positively swear by Mercedes-Benz. We've had less-than-list, no-money-down deal with them for years. Our position is that any omniscient Being would, ipso facto, know about our little arrangement and talk to us first."

TODAY'S THOUGHT FROM THE BIBLE

"And he inquired unto Eliphaz the Terminate, Does this look infected to you?"
-The Book of Jobs 17:7

St. Stubby the Stew-Giver Holiday Inspiration for the Ages

REV. BERT STEWARD Jr
Religion Editor

Many a time, especially as the festive season approaches, I have wondered what I would do if, like Stubby of Tours in anno domini 1136, I had been besieged by 14,000 crazed Albuquerquian heretics in a tiny bingo hall just off rue Principal in downtown Tours?

The ramparts were mighty, yea, and they could not be breached by the insistent multitudes. And yet Stubby and his 11 followers were without victuals of any description.

For the next nine months they managed as best they could, mostly by eating each other's whips, hairshirts, and scabs.

By the feast day of St. Olaf the Frottagist in the summer of 1137, Stubby knew that unless he and his naked flock ate soon they would not live to see the feast day of St. Boleslaw the Flatulent the following weekend.

St. Olaf's Day dawned, and Stubby prayed, as he had every day during his confinement, for a sign from heaven. Suddenly, a large kohlrabi fell out of the sky and struck Stubby at the base of the skull. When he awoke he found he could speak fluent Urdu, albeit with a French accent.

After several hours of meditation, Stubby concluded that although Urdu was nice to have, it would not help him and his followers out of their current predicament. Nor would one serving from the vegetable food group provide a balanced meal for those under siege.

Suddenly, Stubby knew what he had to do. With a dull bit of rusted eaves-troughing, he removed all his protruding and dangling body parts and added them to the kohlrabi to make a nice, nourishing stew.

The Stubbyites ate heartily and, with their newfound strength, they fled, simply outrunning the opposition and leaving the limbless Stubby to face the music by himself. The Albuquerquians, having devoted nine months to the operation, were sorely irked. What they did to poor Stubby cannot be described in the pages of a family newspaper, especially the bit about the rabid gerbil.

Stubby of Tours was canonized by Pope Jerry III in 1597.

As this holiday season approaches, I often wonder would I, under similar circumstances, have performed the same selfless act as this simple peasant who became St. Stubby the Stew-Giver?

I think not.

Announcements

BOOKS

QUIK READS

- **The Question of Being** by Martin Heidegger. Ideal for boat or cottage, this is about philosophy in the truest sense. (Of that X word.) A master work by the ace prof who lived quite a long time ago in Germany. Some say Heidegger was a Nazi but you can't tell this from the work under review although he did speak in German a good deal of the time.

- **The Idiot** by Fydor Dostoevsky. An early examination of the split personality which we hear a lot about these days, mostly from television and the movies, although it was not so well known about when the great Communist novelist wrote it up. A bit wordy.

- **The Diary of Vaslav Nijinksy.** Ed. Romola Nijinsky. Not only for the tutu set, these diaries are fascinating and give us a fascinating glimpse into the artistic life of a man who played hard, danced hard and died hard. Fascinating.

- **Lytton Strachey** by Michael Holroyd (two volumes). Lytton Strachey was a writer in his own right and biographer Holroyd does the eminent Victorian proud. (Interestingly, Strachey wrote a book called Eminent Victorians!) There is no evidence that Strachey ever met Nijinsky, the great Russian dancer and *bon vivant*, which is a pity because they would have probably got on reasonably well. Holroyd pulls no punches as he shows us the warts and everything, of which there were many (warts) in those times because of the lack of advances in medicine not like now.

- **The Critique of Judgement** by Immanuel Kant. Welcome reissue of an all-time fave by the gloomy German penseur who gave us the ding an sich. Not much about Canada. A timely reminder.

Debbie Coyne's Odyssey

Out From Under The Alabaster-Loined Icon

Yes! Yes!! Oh, God, Pierre, Yes!!! The Autobiography of Deborah Coyne, as told to Charlotte Gray, Vol. III: The Turbulent Years (Red Stocking Collective, P. O. Box 2, Sta. "A" The Glebe, Ottawa), $122.95 before Oct. 26; $2.95 after.

By Camille Pagliarulo

Previous volumes in this epochal autobiography have detailed the details of the sparse—in the Althuserrian sense—upbringing that Debbie had under a severe father-figure. The patriarchical Dr. Coyne, a life-long smoker, instilled the fear of God (a white male with a beard, that very follicular signifier mentioned by Julie Kristeva and Gloria Steinem) and allowed Debbie only one month annually at Gstaad. (There's a lot of pain in this book.)

The unfortunate oral incontinence that plagues Debbie and causes her to salivate on television is fearlessly faced up to here: she rightly blames this embarrassing spittle-ridden flatulence on the atmosphere induced by the linear-minded phallicism of the bourgeois-patriarchal mode of late capitalism that affected her traumatically during those early formative years. "It is," she declares, "the saliva, that is, in its own inchoate way, a cry for help."

But what a change in Volume III! This book could be called "Out from Under." Starting from the pink ghetto of cooking recipes on local CBC radio in St. John's, Debbie moved assuredly and with grace to the Maudie Barlow Hour and then to the mystery guest on Guess Who I Am? with Betty Kennedy.

When Clyde Wells wanted to find out something about constitutional theory, Debbie offered herself. "Do you ever take that vest off?" she challenged him nonchalantly at their first meeting.

The rest is history. Her relationship with Pierre Trudeau is handled with great tact and reserve: she tells us, interestingly enough, that he has in fact a quite small member. (So much for those old husband stories about little dogs having long tails!)

When she and the alabaster-loined icon finally consummate their relationship, Debbie insisted on being on top. In this regard, it is interesting to note how heavily the referendum question weighed on her mind even during this essentially existential moment. (And yet further evidence just how political the personal is!)

... then I asked him with my eyes to ask again yes and then he asked me would I say yes to say yes my mountain flower and first I put my arms around him yes and drew him down so he could feel my breasts all perfume yes and his heart was going like mad and yes I said yes yes I will yes...

This is really good writing on Debbie's part. Clearly she is a role model for all young women all over the whole world. Not at all like that foreign papist bitch married to the big mick living in 24 Sussex these days. (But not for long, eh?)

(Camille Pagliarulo is with the Rising Up Angry Red Stocking Collective at Carleton University's Wimmins Program.)

BOOKS

TURD SKEWERED
Citizen book editor

COVER TO COVER

PAPERBAX

The Ornate Newell Post by Lydia MacKinnon. Onan Press, P. O. Box 24, Sta. "A", Carp. Ont. Her many fans have been waiting for this one by Lydia MacKinnon. It's a shame her previous 42 books are currently out of print. In this one, the heroine Agnes Farquhar is rummaging through her grandmother's old trunk in the attic and finds a lot of letters tied together with a blue ribbon. They introduce her to a world about which she could scarcely and only dimly guess about. The atmosphere of Post is beautifully caught in a filigree web leading inexorably to a diapason as well as an epiphany in the truest sense. Like Lytton Strachey, MacKinnon uses words to achieve her effects, the best of which would remind a person of the sunlight filtering through the birches on a crisp day in late Fall near Carp or Smith Falls or anywhere really in the National Capital Region. (Some violence.) (Also some smoking.)

-Agnes Farquhar
(Agnes is a bookseller in Carp, Ont.)

How to make your marriage last...and last by Megan Schultz-O'Flaherty-Dupuis-Boggs. Alimony Books, Barrhaven, Ont. This timely guide to relationships takes the reader through the twelve steps required for a stable and nurturing relationship. The author, who is herself a marriage counsellor, leaves no holds barred. (She even mentions dirty socks!) Schultz-O'Flaherty-Dupuis-Boggs is very good on "denial." Definitely a "must" for that "significant other" in your life and a pleasant change of "pace" from the Constitution and everything.

-Jim Boggs
(Jim Boggs is a marriage counsellor living full-time in Barrhaven, Ont.)

◀ **That Goal!** by Paul Henderson. Illustrated, with pop-up hockey cards. McGill-Queens University Press. This is a ffucking great book.

-Dayv James Ffrench
(Dayv James-Ffrench lives with his mum in her house.)

Spy Stinker Sinks

Chris Tide Lays A Million Dollar Egg

Bomb! by Chris Tide. Berlusconi Enterprises, Scarborough. Soon to be in a video outlet near you.

Turd Skewered

O ttawa and the National Capital Region novelist Chris Tide's new novel is quite explosive. In an interview in his gracious home, Tide brushed aside a visitor's query about the $160 million (Can.) advance from Berlusconi Export-Import of Palermo, his new publisher. "I brush that aside," declared the life-long non-smoker, a line he repeated at a hushed press conference at Patti's Place in Vanier last week.

Like Dostoevsky, Tide sets his scene in St. Petersburg, where Igor Oistrakh, ex-KGB agent and now conducting his Palm Court Orchestra in Santa Barbara, California (where, interestingly, John Steinbeck used to set some of his scenes, or at least nearby), is pining for Barbara, a British film actress whose dying mother is still alive in Nottingham, where D. H. Lawrence, the well-known writer (Travels in Italy), used to set scenes.

Barbara's mother, once a member of the British Communist Party, remarried Luigi Pirandello, a Milanese sculptor now living in Rome (where Iris Murdoch set some scenes and where Gore Vidal, who was in a film recently, now lives).

The question Chris Tide raises: who has the Bomb? And what will they do with it?

Tide uses words with considerable skill.

Memories of Calumet Island by Myrtle and Wilbur Fitzroy-Harbour. Deep Hollow Press, General Store, Barrie, Ont. (No price.)

Keith Bilious

O stensibly a collection of oral history accounts of 19-century Ottawa Valley working class types, social mores, logging, that kind of thing, what one finds here is syntagmatic construction that survives, paradoxically, by its own denial. (Icarus springs to mind.) Metaphor here becomes, one intuits, a flirtatious whore, mediated by tropes more latent than holistic, with no correspondence between signifier and signified. The Fitzroy-Harbours have laboured, so to speak, in vain: fragmentation and discontinuity become transvalued in the intensification of associative relationships.

Pity really.
(Keith Billious is the acting chairperson of the University of Ottawa's English Dept.)

M argaret Atwood's wry yet dry humour was the pièce de resistance of the Gloucester Writer's Conference. It was held in Gloucester. Atwood was not able to attend but conferencers were able to see and hear her read her new haiku (a short Japanese-type poem, although not really allied with karaoke) on closed-circuit television for them.

Since the pint-sized poem will be published (illustrations by Gnu, the well-known Australian lithographer) in time for the Christmas trade, I can't reprint it here. But here's a teaser: the last line is "not many leaves on the forest floor." (Black Moss Publishers, Kleinburg, Ont.) Send money.

The House of Speculative Fiction (105 4th Ave., the Glebe) continues its interesting speculative fiction series with Megan Bogs' Eastern Ontario-West Quebec Gothic oeuvre, Trick or Trunk? In it, the heroine, Vale del Monte, is going through her grandmother's trunk in the attic and finds a deadly secret that the family wanted hushed up until now.

It makes you think.

Kathryn Firehall's latest book of poems deals with native themes in a deep way that makes Kevin Costner look shallow. (By comparison.) A sample:

Get out the sweet
grass
Let the healing
process
Begin

It's interesting how Kathryn breaks the sentences up into munch-sized pieces. T. S. Eliot tried this too but not nearly to the same degree. Kathryn will read from her "When moon rise over tree you die slow death" before the Bingo game at the Orange Hall, Shawville, at 8 p.m. Monday, Nov. 22. (Cash bar.)

HIGH priority

HIGH ON LIFE!
Today's teens face difficult choices

Jimmy Page
Citizen teen science writer

Good one on the name, huh? High Priority. If you go to Bell like I did, High is definitely a Priority, if you know what I mean.

I wouldn't have got booted out if the vice principal wasn't such a liar—there was like no way I'd have an ounce in my locker at one time.

I told the guy, "I know the law, man." But he threatened to call the cops if I didn't turn it over to him. He probably sold it or used it in his soup, the beaner.

And that stuff about me shaking down that Grade 9 kid is like total bullshit. I'm sure I'm gonna roll some geeky little dweeb for two bucks milk money. Anyway, you think Pearl Jam tickets grow on trees? Oh, yeah, another thing. The driver's ed teacher's daughter? Never went near her. She wanted me to, though, y'know, cause when that Helmut guy had a party when his parents went to Germany and she saw me roll the projection TV into the pool, she didn't say anything, so that thing about the phone calls can't be true. Same goes for her puking in the lab—it was her idea to drink the stuff they put the frogs in. A dare is a dare, I say.

Also, the consumer ed teacher was totally biased against me ever since that incident with the paint job on his Range Rover. My proposal for the Doc Marten resale business was a dynamic, commercially-viable enterprise. I only got an F because he was jealous that he didn't think of it first.

But today's teenagers face difficult choices. I'm glad I got kicked out cause I'm doing real well for myself as a direct marketing representative.

It's a pretty cool job. I get to boot around these office buildings selling athletic socks door to door. You meet a lot of receptionists, if only for a few seconds.

I remember last week I was on the elevator and there was this one who...

(That's enough essays—ed.)

Boyfriend should first examine the risks

Dear Dr. Levine: Say you had like, you know, a thing on your, you know, thing, and it really hurt when the dog licked it? Would that be bad?

Dr. Levine replies:
Today's teenagers are often confused by conflicting messages about their sexuality. At school and in the home, they are warned about the risks of pregnancy and sexually transmitted diseases, but at the same time, film and television bombards them with images that seem to encourage promiscuity. Rock videos aimed at teenagers exploit sex to sell records, especially that one where the

DR. SAUL LEVIATHAN   **DR. DIANE SACKED**

YOUTH CLINIC

blonde woman with the latex hangs by her wrists over the drum kit. If you use the pause and frame advance just right, you can almost see her right nipple. Boy, that gets me hot. And that Madonna woman! Yow! You kids today are very fortunate. When I went to school, our idea of a sex symbol was Janis Joplin—and she couldn't give a doberman a boner! If this doesn't answer your question, consult your family doctor.

Dear Dr. Sacks: Can you die from acne? I bet a friend of mine a pint of alcool that you could.

Dr. Sacks replies: Today's teenagers are very concerned about their personal appearance, sometimes needlessly so. My daughter, for instance—you should see the outfits. $180 for a miniskirt! Marsha, I said, for what is the $180? It barely covers your tush. Are you mashuge? But this is what the kids are wearing. Now she wants a different colour cell phone to match her suede jacket.

Dear Dr. Levine: What's this masturbation thing I've been hearing so much about? It sounds great!

Dr. Levine replies: Get some help, you sicko.

(Young readers are invited to write to Dr. Levine and Dr. Sacks c/o the Ottawa Citizen. Include a recent photograph, if possible. Anonymity is guaranteed, except for that first letter which is from J. Thompson of RR1, Nepean.)

WHAT TO DO AT THE PLACE TO BE

CANADIAN MUSEUM OF CRIMINALIZATION EVENTS & ACTIVITIES

PHONY WAR
Theatre
To Fall, 1992

Showtimes: At 11 a.m., Noon, and 1 p.m. Phoney War, a spectacular fantasy which celebrates bluster and ego. With its special reports and outstanding song and dance, this colourful constitutional battle just won't go away. For politicians of all ages. Tickets are available at the Museum Box Office or the Tory Quebec Caucus. $5,000. Bilingual for now.

SPECIAL EVENTS
MICHEL COGGER AND HENRY JENSEN
Supreme Court
February 1991 - 1993

A Quebec businessman who just happens to be a personal friend of the Prime Minister, and a key fundraiser for the PC Party of Canada, Senator Michel Cogger was a highlight of the Museum's opening festivities and gained great popularity with Mounties after miffed business partners squealed. A shy man, he has agreed to relive his memorable role, but only if the taxpayer picks up the tab. Cogger and many interesting characters bring you a richly varied body of testimony and accusation incorporating many traditional legends and newspaper clippings.

SITE ANIMATION
February 14, 1991, between 1 and 4 p.m.

The museum recalls its colourful past by presenting a unique, fun-filled animation programme. Small payments to colourful Tory insiders will elicit information and interesting documents that should guide you through the system. Sit through colourful presentations such as: Knock, Knock with Mario Taddeo, Vroom Vroom Boom with Henri Paquin, We'll Take a Cheque and Eat Up Boys with Roch La Salle, a serpentine trail that leads nowhere because nobody did anything wrong. Also listen and watch as a life-like Michel Gravel quietly pleads guilty to fraud and influence peddling after being innocent for 2 years.

CHANGING EXHIBITIONS
THE MILA MULDOON POTTERY
1984 - 1990
Arts and Traditions Hall
To March 1, 1992

The ceramics of Mila Mulroney, which she picked out with her former chef François Martin from National Arts Centre catalogues, then ordered and innovatively inserted into the bills for official functions. The exhibition features up to 70 place settings given to friends, along with official presentation cards and thank-you notes.

OUT OF TOUCH
THE PMO IN CANADA
Special Exhibitions Hall
To February 19, 1991

An exhibition of hundreds of Mulroneyite artifacts based on the recollections of the many men and women who have served the country so well over the past 6 years. Included are Mr. Bonnie Brownlee's forged expense accounts, reams of unacknowledged phone messages, and unread briefing books prepared for The Honourable Tom Siddon. Visitors of all ages can test their memory and skill by trying to recall what exactly it *was* that Dalton Camp did before returning to *The Toronto Star*.

CHILDREN'S MUSEUM
WHERE'S MULDOON?
Kaleidoscope
To March 1, 1991

Children will have loads of fun as they search through the giant pages of Terry Mosher's popular game book, looking for the elusive Muldoon. The nation is about to go to War in Arabia, the First Nations are on the Warpath on the St. Lawrence River, and Quebec is about to secede. Can you find the Prime Minister? No one else could. Related programmes and games will encourage children to believe what they are told by the government, but still laugh at funny pictures they don't quite understand (in conjunction with The Canadian Centre For Caricature, located somewhere in the National Capital Region.)

FAMILY TREASURES
Kaleidoscope
To March 1, 1991

Children will be delighted with this reconstruction of the basement at 24 Sussex. They can scamper among boxes of corporate gifts, stocks of gifts waiting to be recycled on Party members and unlucky dignitaries, and the dump of presents sent by unmonied average Canadians. .

PARLIAMENT will reopen February 21, 1991 so school groups can see future Museum exhibits in action.

OPEN TUESDAYS TO SUNDAYS, FROM 9 A.M. TO 5 P.M., THURSDAYS UNTIL 8 P.M.

CANADIAN MUSEUM   MUSÉE CANADIEN
OF CRIMINALIZATION DES CRIMINALIZATION

100 Laurier Street, Box 3100, Station B. Hull, Quebec J8X 4H2 **(819) 776-7000**

See you at the PMO

SUN

25

April Paid Circulation: never mind   THURSDAY, MAY 2, 1991   ~~56~~ ~~42~~ 29 PAGES

SADDAM IN GAY LOVER STORM

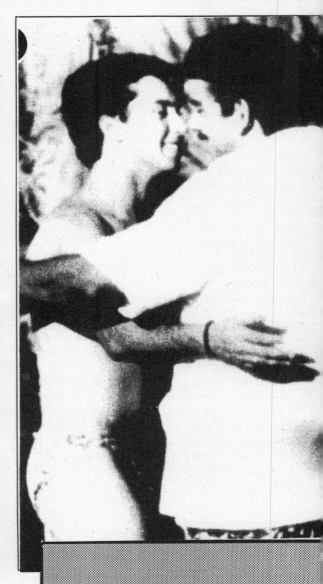

Iraq's Saddam Hussein embrace
his gay lover at their luxurious
palace hide-away in Greece.

photo: david phieg

Saddam's nights of gay bonking

Sun/CBS Exclusive— Furious Moslems last night accused the Pentagon of a Gay Smear campaign against Iraq's Saddam Hussein.

The diplomatic row was touched off by the publication of intimate photos— allegedly showing Hussein relaxing with his Toyboy. The pictures, seen in Canada for the first time in today's Sun, were apparently taken at a Greek island love-nest in July by Sun ace war correspondent Tim Numbnutz.

But Moslems claim the pictures were part of a CIA smear campaign to discredit the Iraqi president.

An Iraqi source denied Saddam is gay and said, "This is an outrage against Allah and those responsible will feel His wrath."

Sun publisher Doug Creighton responded, "...and hold the olive."

JEFF BASSOON'S

SUNshine Boy

There's nothing Bob likes better than donning a hard hat, getting sweaty and throwing around some lunch pails. He can be seen boogying his buns in the Provincial Legislature everyday (except Sunday).

GARY DUMPFORD

KNOCK, KNOCK
Who's there?
Me again.
Me again, who?
The pathetic Yank scribbler Barbara Amiel should have fired when she had the chance.
***
A LOT MORE FUNNY STUFF
Do you file your nails?
No, I cut them off and throw them away.
How do you stop an Iraqi tank?
Shoot the two guys pushing it.
What's the national bird of Iraq?
Duck.
Why's the Scud such a popular cocktail?
Drink as many as you want, then drive home. You can't hit anything.
Name the only surviving rock band in Kuwait.
No Kids on the Block.
They've added oat bran to Rice Krispies.
Snap, Crackle, Poop.
(Okay, okay, fuck off. That's enough Dumpford for now.—ed.)

SUSAN BIRD

Big Hubby Mandarin *(we know it's you Hartley so quit, already—ed.)* spotted several prominent government officials making illegal left turns in front of the Langevin Block. Tsk, tsk. I won't name names, since I never do, but you have been warned, fellas.

*   *   *

At McGinnis Landing roadhouse, Susie got a little tired and emotional *(dated euphemism, lost on incontinent SUN readers—ed.)* with a nameless SUN publisher who we'll call...well, we won't call him anything. Anyway, he drove and Susie saw him make an illegal left turn onto Highway 16. Tsk, tsk. You have been warned, H.

WAR BUSINESS REVIEW

SOUVENIR WAR ISSUE

NOVEMBER 29, 1990 • EVERY TWO WEEKS • ISSUE 77

WAR

BUSINESS REVIEW

WE'RE NOT JUST FIGHTING SUDDAM HUSSEIN, WE'RE FIGHTING THE RECESSION!

CANADIAN BUSINESS AND CANADIAN TECHNOLOGY BUCK THE RECESSION.

IT WON'T BE LONG TIL JOHNNY COMES MARCHING HOME--HOME TO A COUNTRY OF SNIVELLING, RECESSION-PANICKED AGORAPHOBICS! TAKE HEART CANADA! LOOK TO THE EXAMPLES OF GET-UP-AND-GO IN THESE PAGES AND PULL YOURSELVES TOGETHER. REMEMBER THAT EVERY CANADIAN KIA IN THE GULF IS CREATING A JOB OPENING IN THE ARMED FORCES.

NATO NO. C.A. III-396-0522
UNITS ON ORDER: 250

COMBAT ACCORDION

THE POLKAMAX 100

IN THE GULF CRISIS THE WORLD FAMOUS "COMBAT ACCORDIANISTS" WILL EMPLOY THE STATE-OF-THE-ART POLKAMAX 100 ARMOURED ACCORDION. THIS RUGGED CLASSIC IS PRODUCED BY SCHMENGEWERKE OF NEW KIEV, ALTA. UNITS OF THE ROYAL UKRANIAN REGIMENT, THE PRINCESS PEROGIES, HAVE BEEN TRAINING SINCE AUGUST AT THE "LIVE MUSIC PROVING RANGE" IN NEW KIEV. THE POLKAMAX 100 FEATURES A LIGHTWEIGHT TITANIUM SHELL WITH BALLISTIC NYLON BELLOWS AND IS DESERT-MODIFIED WITH FILTERED AIR BREATHERS, AND A SELF-LUBRICATING KEYBOARD.

YOUNG MEN GO, OLD MEN RETURN

"WAR IS HECK," SAYS 19-YEAR-OLD MARVIN 'THE KID' COONEY OF TORONTO. "I SAW UNSPEAKABLE HORRORS, ATROCITIES PERFORMED WITH HOMMUS AND HAND HOLDING. I HEARD COUNTRY AND EASTERN MUSIC. I SAW TWO IRAQIS TAKING A DUMP TOGETHER ON A BEACH WHILE HOLDING...HOLDING...HA...HANDS! I JUST CAN'T TALK ABOUT IT ANYMORE."
OUR BOYS WILL BE COMING HOME WITH INVISIBLE WAR WOUNDS, THE KIND THAT WILL SOMEDAY LEAD THEM, AK-47 IN HAND, TO THE SIDEWALK SALE AT BAYSHORE SHOPPING CENTRE.

19-YEAR-OLD "KID" COONEY OF THE ROYAL CANADIAN REGIMENT

INFLATABLE INFANTRY

"THEY REALLY GO OFF WITH A HELL OF A SHOT," SAYS MARCEL RACETTE, SPOKESTHINGY FOR LOVE TECHNOLOGIES, MAKERS OF CANADA'S NEW PNEUMATIC COMMANDO.
CANADA'S VISIBILITY CAN BE TRIPLED OVERNIGHT AT A REASONABLE COST. LOVE TECH IS WORKING ON AN INFLATABLE SAILOR WITH HANDLES THAT DOUBLES AS A LIFE PRESERVER.

NATO NO. IC -0168
UNITS ORDERED: 10,000

MONUMENTAL EFFORT

DANISH-BORN ENTREPRENEUR AND LAWN ORNAMENT PHENOM LARS HANSEN OF PORCHMONKI, N.B., HAS ANTICIPATED THE OBVIOUS NEED FOR INEXPENSIVE MUNICIPAL WAR MONUMENTS ONCE THE DUST HAS SETTLED IN THE GULF.
"WITH 3,000 CANADIAN COMMUNITIES TO SERVICE, WE'VE GOT ENOUGH WORK HERE TO MAKE US ALL ELIGIBLE FOR UIC AGAIN," SAYS LARS.

NATO NO. MM-572-2609
UNITS ORDERED: 4,000

PLEASE SPECIFY "KNEELING," "PRONE," OR "GRENADE TOSS" POSITIONS

FAMILY BROWN SEES GREEN

LEGENDARY FIRST FAMILY OF COUNTRY AND WESTERN, THE FAMILY BROWN, HAVE REUNITED TO TOUR THE GULF REGION. "WE'VE HAD TO GO BACK ON THE ROAD TO RAISE CASH TO SUPPORT OUR $2,000-A-DAY NUTRASYSTEM HABIT," SAYS DRUMMER BARRY-BOB BROWN.

 CANADIAN RECYCLED DEFENSE PROGRAM

STILL LOOKS MODERN!

BOMARC LIVES

If it was good enough to defend Canada, then surely it's good enough to defend Arabs!

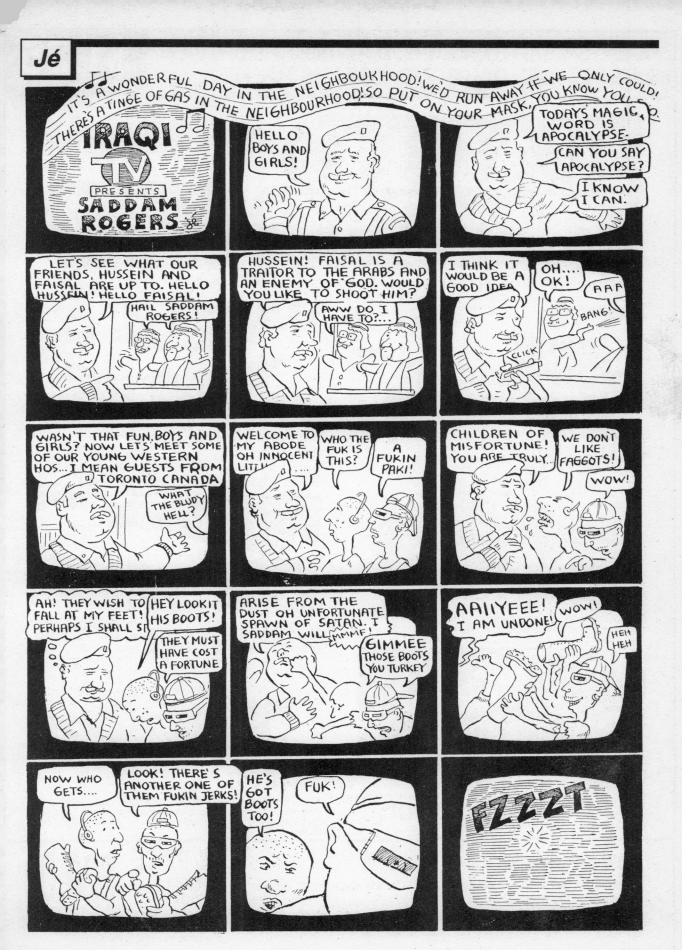

THE CANADIAN MIXED DANCE FLOOR CLEARING CHAMPION.

IN THIS EVENT, COMPETITORS CONSUME MIND-BENDING QUANTITIES OF ALCOHOL AND ATTEMPT TO CLEAR A TEN-FOOT RADIUS ON A CROWDED DANCE FLOOR WHILE TEAMMATES YELL BOOZY ENCOURAGEMENT FROM THE SIDELINES. SOME CLASSIC MOVES ARE THE ELBOW-TO-CHEST ARM SWING, THE OVER-THE-HEAD DRAFT DUMP, AND THE MOUTHFUL O' SUDS AIRBORNE FACIAL. PROVIDED THEIR OPPONENTS WEIGH LESS THAN 120-LBS. COMPETITORS IN THE 235-LB. CRUISERWEIGHT DIVISION MAY ATTEMPT THE REVERSED ASSAULT CHARGE, BUT SHOULD CONSULT EXPENSIVE LEGAL ADVICE BEFOREHAND.

MOLSON CANADIAN

CLEAN, COLD AND...HEY, GET THE FUCK OUTA MY WAY, HONEY

Beach Blanket Bingo

I see a red whore
And I want to paint him black
No pinkos anymore
I want them to turn back

You say you want a constitution
Well you know
We're all impacting what we're mandated

Boors lose votes
And dopes lose votes
And Premier Bob knows diddly

Summertime
And meat makes me queasy
Ranchers are jumpy
But soy futures are high

My boyfriend's bald
And you're going to be sorry
Hey la dee la
My boyfriend's bald

"By way of Deception"
Has dubious spies
But I've got a wallet
As thick as my thighs

WAKE UP EVERYBODY! IT'S TIME FOR PETER GZOWSKI'S

MORNINGSLIDE

..6 TWEET TWEET

...IN HOUR TWO WE'LL VISIT WITH THE RADISH LADY OF RED DEER AND IN HOUR THREE WE'LL CHAT WITH THE CHAMPION YO-YO EATER FROM THE NATIONAL CAPITAL-HULL REGION BUT FIRST,...SOMETHING QUITE EXTRAORDINARY....

I PIG MY NOZ

HEH-HEH HOW POPULIST OF YOU! AND YET... AND YET... I'M JUST HOPELESS AT PIGGING MY NOZ AS YOU SO REGIONALLY PUT IT. I REMEMBER, AS A YOUNG BOY IN GALT....

I STIG MY FINGE IN MY NOZ.

I NEARLY POKED OUT MY EYE WITH A MISDIRECTED DIGITAL THRUST. YOU WON'T GET ME TO DO THAT AGAIN, NO SIR! ALTHOUGH IT BRINGS TO MIND A SINGULAR....

IDZ STUCK!

INCIDENT WHEN I WAS SAILING MY YACHT SINGLE HANDED EXCEPT FOR NORTHERN DANCER AND ED SCHREYER, THE DEAN OF CANADIAN..

NNNGH!

GOVERNORS GENERAL. I'M A HOPELESS SAILOR AND JUS AS THE MAINMAST BROKE, I WAS REMINDED OF MY COMPLETE INEPTNESS AT PLAYING LEFT—

UUUUH!

WING FOR THE EDMONTON OILERS. AS WAYNE GRETZKY, THE DEAN OF CANADIAN GEEKS, ONCE SAID TO MY GOOD FRIEND SNIFFY THE RAT, THE DEAN OF CANADIAN RODENTS.

MMMF!

THIS VAST COUNTRY HAS A VASTNESS ABOUT IT THAT IS TRULY VAST AND WHY, IN THE SWEET SUNNY NEWFOUNDLAND MORNINGS, DO THE LOBSTERS ROLL WITH THE..

OOOG!

TUMBLING, TUMESCENT TIDES? IF ONLY WE, AS CANADIANS, COUL WOULD, AND FACE THE REAL THING... AND YET....AND YET AND...

BANG!

SO!.. YOU'RE THE MAYOR OF ATHABASKA! I ADMIRE THE MOOSE POOP COOKBOOK. WHEN IS YOUR HOUSING PRICE COMING DOWN? WHAT IS THE WATERSHED FOR THE N.D.P.? ARE WE IN A...

?

CRISIS OR IS IT TRUE THAT THE CRISIS ITSELF IS AT THE CRITICAL CROSSROADS? IS THE STABILITY OF THE SOVIET UNION WORTH A CHIPMUNK? I DON'T EVER WEAR A SUIT AS I DON'T AP... T... LB!

I STIG MY FINGA IN MY EAR.

IS STEVEN LEWIS A CLIMBING LIZARD? IS THE G.S.T. BIGGER THA THE FREE TRADE OR HAVE THEY BEEN INFLATED BY THE DEAN OF CANADIAN INTEREST RATES? I'M JUST A HOPELESS ETC. ETC.

WILL IT NEVER END

$2.75

THE NATIONAL
Radio • Guide

JANUARY LISTINGS FOR CBC RADIO AND CBC STEREO

LORNE GREEN

OUR VOICE
IN THE GULF

DEAD MEN WORK CHEAP

25

RADIO

6.13 AM
LOCAL PROGRAM
Ottawa Host: Bert Bodkin
Bert plays a WW I ditty and describes frost patterns on the seventh-floor windows at the Chateau Laurier.

7.00 am
LOCAL PROGRAM
Ottawa: CBO Morning
Host: John LaCharitycase
Including: objects found in Stittsville sewers; Malvina Roofrack blithers on about the Nepean Alzheimer Theatre Society's production of something or other; Cameron Fraser stumbles through last week's ringette scores.

9.05 am
BORINGSIDE
Host: Peter Gzzzzzzzi
Peter unctuously pretends to envy the lifestyle of yet another mental defective from Shrivel, Sask., who's convinced it's the best darned place in the world to live in; Stephen Clueless out-enunciates Dalton Cramp and Eric Alsoran in an exchange of tedious political sermons; Peter treats some aging ninth-rate alcoholic pederast of a Canadian stage actor with a preposterously phony British accent who hasn't worked since a 1969 production of The Fantastics at the Thunder Bay Bowlodrome Dinner Theatre as an equal of

Olivier; Stuart MacLame rhapsodizes for what seems like two hours about belly-button lint; Jolleigh Rogers reveals embarrassing things about herself while giggling her way through some incredibly long-winded and stunningly pointless letters from listeners who got new thesauruses for Christmas all the while trying to undo Peter's fly with her foot; the Boringside drama continues with episode three of Sunshine Sketches of a Little Town performed entirely in Yiddish.

12 Noon
RADIO NOON
Ottawa Host: Rob Wimperton
Mary Cook tells tales of incest and bestiality in the Ottawa Valley; an interview with the manager of the Ontario Head Cheese Marketing Board; roadkill recipes; today's phone-in topic: udder rot in goats.

2.05 pm
BLABEREAU
Host: Vicki Blabereau
Vicki sucks up to the long-

time companion of the same aging ninth-rate alcoholic pederast of a Canadian stage actor with a preposterously phony British accent who hasn't worked since a 1969 production of The Fantastics at the Thunder Bay Bowlodrome Dinner Theatre who was just on the Gzzzzzzzi show this morning.

4.05 pm
LOCAL PROGRAM
Ottawa: All in a Daze
Host: Jennifer Fried
Charles Staines wheezes and hawks his way through a review of the Centretown Lesbian Thespian Coalition's production of Les Ms.; Tommy Flanagan-McCarthy in the CBO Mobile files three reports on a stuck exit gate at the Chateau Laurier parking garage; syndicated lifestyles commentator Nils Thing tells us all about the latest craze, the lambada; Peter Poofter reviews Ottawa's cutest waiters.

6.00 pm
THE WHIRLED AT SIX
With Alannah Oxley and Bob Campbell

Alannah and Bob talk to each other about the Gulf.

6.30 pm
AS IT YAPPINS
Host: Michael Gumright
Ed McMahon: Alan Maitland
More twice-as-long-as necessary interviews to make whatever the hell the pinko point was using semi-audible phone hook-ups with people with thick accents.

8.05 pm
LAME TIME
Host: Geoff Peever, age 9
Um, Geoff, um, introduces, um, more interviews on the, um, inane and inconsequential aspects of, um, popular culture, as if he's, um, explaining, um, bed-making to the, um, slow-learner's cabin.

9.05 pm
IKEAS
Host: Fister Sinclair
In a plummy accent that exists nowhere in the English-speaking world, Fister discusses the concept of assemble-yourself furniture from Aristotle through Seneca to Hegel and Nils Bilbo.

PET PEEVES OF THE ANNOUNCERS

"You know what really puts a knot in my vocal chords?" says veteran CBC newsreader Dougall W. McDougall. "It's when the CBC Pronunciation Police changes its friggin' mind in mid-stream, which it's always doing, thank you very much. There you are droning through the news, your mind drifting off to that pitcher of very dry martinis with your name on it in the announcers' lounge fridge, and suddenly, there it is, like Khomeini, and you gotta stop and think, 'What the friggin' hell is it this week? KOMENI, HOMENI, HORKMENI?' Who the hell can remember? Make up your friggin' mind, why don't you? 'Ko-ME-ni, HO-me-ni, Hork-on-my KNEE?' Man, I was one happy talking head, let me tell you, when that old fart died. But, no, they had to go droppin' the friggin' coffin and there you go, another friggin' Ayatollah story to read. "And another thing that really ticks me off while I'm at it. It's when...

FARTS NATIONAL'S QUACKERJACK HOST

"I'm absolutely thrilled to be doing what I'm doing," says Farts National host Howard the Duck in his feathery-soft baritone. "To think they actually pay me to sit in a swivel chair and listen to Swan Lake just blows my mind." Howard, who was hatched sounding exactly like he does now, first aspired to a career as a television anchor. "It was Knowlton Nash who inspired me when I was a mere duckling in this business," he says. "I figured if a guy with a mug like a frog could make it, there was no reason why I couldn't. I always expected him to slip up some night and wrap that big sticky tongue of his around a fly instead of a syllable. 'Kermit,' we always called him behind his back." And it was precisely because of this sobriquet that Howard found himself exiled to radio. "It all turned out for the best, really," he says. "They handed me Farts National and let me sink or swim with it. I'm happy to say it's where I found my wings."

10.08 pm
THE BEST OF BORINGSIDE
Host: Peter Gzzzzzzzzi

11.08 pm
THAT TIME OF THE MONTH
Host: Peter Tonight
Tonight's highlight: Sans-Sen: Symphonie insensible, Orchestre Symphonique de Montreal (Charles Dutwat)

STEREO

5.00 am
STEREO MOURNING
The dreary way to start the day.

9.05 am
MUSTY MUSIC
Host: Ken Twinkie
Twinkie pretends to broadcast live from pre-recorded concerts. Please indulge him.

11.05 am
RSVP
Host: Peon Cole
The toughest job in showbiz—Cole plays your mind-numbing requests.

1.05 pm
OFF THE DEEP END
Host: Bob Cur
Between the lesser works of 17th-century Walloon glockenspiel composers and the chants of Bulgarian sheep buggerers, Cur gets rabid about sloppy liner notes.

3.05 pm
DISCDRIVEL
Host: Jerkin Visigoth
Every weekday at 3:04, Visigoth blows into the studio and without so much as a howdy-do grabs the ad libs his researchers have prepared for him and starts winging through them as he introduces a lobotomizing blend of elevator and wallpaper music, one selection of which is almost guaranteed to be a soggy instrumental rendition of Fool on the Hill. During musical interludes, Visigoth augments his puny CBC salary by tossing off a few annual reports for corporate clients, scribbling the odd wine review, and sampling the not-so-odd bottle of wine. When he gets really cranked, Visigoth will often toss his prepared asides and read liner notes backwards, or prattle on and on about his ex-cats who now reside with his ex-wife. Unaccountably popular even to us.

6.00 pm
THE WHIRLED AT SIX

6.30 pm
THE AHTS TONIGHT
Host: Jolleigh Rogers
Ahts interviews and reviews punctuated by blood-curdling cackles from Rogers

7.00 pm
GLISTEN TO THE MUSIC
Host: Angela Crisco

8.05 AT, 8.35 NT
STRING OF PEARLS
Host: Elizabeth II

8.00 pm 9.00 AT, 9.30 NT
FARTS NATIONAL
Host: Howard the Duck
From the Royal Monte Hall in Toronto, a program of modern compositions by Canada's Flatus Wind Ensemble, with guest soloist Fred Pennis.
F. MURRAY ABRAHAM: Symphonie de chou et oeufs marines, op. 911

ORSON BEAN: Le petomane
BRANDO: L'air de feves aux lards
RUMPELSTILTSKIN: Gaz hilarant
Exec. producer: Spuds MacKenzie

10.00 pm
EASY GIG
Not heard AT/NT
Host: Margaret Cashew

11.06 pm
BRAVE NEW WAVES
Host: Bent Bumboy
We don't stay up this late.

26
S A T U R D A Y

RADIO

9.11 am
THE HOUSE AT POOH CORNER
Host: Jim Morrison

10.05 am
BASIC BLACK
Host: Ben Johnson
Featuring people with unusual speech tics and bizarre drug habits.

11.35 am
QUADRUPLE EXPOSURE
A swipe at the week's news and newsmakers, written by and starring Chang and Eng and the Doublemint Twins.

12.08 pm 1.08 NT
NERDS & DORKS
Host: Jay Diagram
A weekly look at what all those spotty, four-eyed geeks with bad B. O. who belonged to your high school chess club are up to now.

FRANK

Peter linked to *Street Legal* star

Mansbridge-Mesley BREAK-UP?

Wendy: seeking revenge

MARCH 5, 1992 · ISSUE 110 · EVERY TWO WEEKS · CENTRAL CANADA FRAN

FRANK

The man who would be a tampon

My kingdom for a Milkbone

Camilla Parker Bow-wow

FEBRUARY 4, 1993 · ISSUE 134   EVERY TWO WEEKS

S KIM CAMPBELL • AL EAGLESON • EVELYN GIGANTES

SEPTEMBER 1990

NUMBER 99 $3.50

CANADA'S MAGAZINE OF EARNEST LIVING

Narrowsmith

METHANE DEBATE: NATURAL OR MAN-MADE

DAVID SUZUKI'S SECRET SHAM

Desktop composting
Cow-pie facials

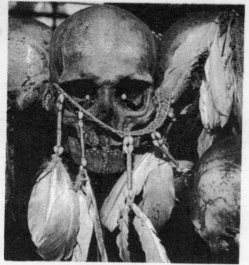

Decorative roach clip holders from
Grandma`s remains 39

Healing with Columbian herbs 94

Is your teenager a zoopheliac? 19

Narrowsmith

Number Ninety-Nine   August `90

FEATURES

SHELTER

GARDENING

COUNTRY LIVING

PANTRY

DEPARTMENTS

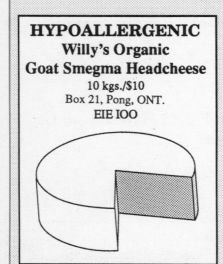

Life in the Glebe

CANADA'S REGURGITATED NEWSMAGAZINE   JULY 26, 1990 $2.25

Maclone's

MURRAY WESTGATE STILL ALIVE

k.d. lang

Real Men Don't Eat Meat

FROM THE EDITOR'S DESK

Lemme Outta Here!

G od, you'd think it'd get easier.
What recycled week-old newspaper clippings can
we run through the old word processor and try to
pass off as news this week?

It's hot. It's muggy. It's mid-July. And I'm certainly not
getting any younger. Sometimes I really despair, you know?

That damn cover story on k. d. lang. I haven't gotten into
such a row with a proof reader since e.e. cummings died.
Lower case, I said, lower case, you idiot!

Oh, forget it. I'm going home.

[signature]

COLUMN

The case for making me a real WASP princess

BY BARBARA SCHLEMIEL

I live in London nowadays where I make fatuous comments on both the British and the Canadian sociopolitical scenes. I abhor statism, especially the Communist brand, because, as anyone with an Eastern European background like myself can tell you, the trains don't run on time. In fact, most of them don't run at all, except when they make one-way trips to the Gulag.

At least, Mussolini made the trains run on time, which would be nice given the state of British Rail these days. Not that I'd ever take the train, mind you.

And not that I'm a huge fan of Mussolini either, even though I firmly

How can the state begin to understand the lust one feels for a young skinhead after squash with Maggie?

believe that at this late date minor functionaries in his service should not be held accountable for minor wartime atrocities. After all, they were only obeying orders — orders given by the state, which, by its very existence, tends all too successfully to remove the rabble from the nexus of individual responsibility.

I hate people telling me what I should

do. What I really enjoy is telling other people what they should do.

I am a Jew. (Did I mention that already?) I play squash with Margaret Thatcher twice a week. She usually wins.

We shower together, along with a few strapping bodyguards. I always marvel at the way the water beads off the Prime Ministerial hair and at the tone with which she barks out orders to her head of security, Rear Adm. St. John-Gumby, as to the proper way to lather a Prime Minister's back.

Afterwards, Mrs. Thatcher and I cruise slowly back to 10 Downing Street in her horse-drawn cabriolet ogling skinheads along the way. We enjoy being conservatives together. But mostly we enjoy being girls together. She delights, as I do, in young heads that look like damp, scarred coconuts. She basks, as I do, in the gleam of their shiny bovver boots.

PEOPLE

TAKE A GANDER AT DEWI

Despite a near-fatal bout of chlamydia, American actress Dewi Tickets has just wrapped shooting on *Slits in the Slammer,* **her first starring role for Scuzz Pictures of Hollywood. What makes Tickets' big-screen debut of special interest to Canadians is the fact that her mother Teri, 27, once dated a U.S. serviceman who stopped over in Gander, Nfld., on a refuelling stop in 1979. Dewi herself told Maclone's she's never heard of Ottawa-born actor Saul Rubinek** *(Ticket to Heaven).* **"Nope, never heard of him," says Dewi. "Still, I have very big breasts for my age." Oh, well, mother teri's Canadian connection will just have to do!**

BUSINESS

CANADIAN BUSINESS FALLS OFF

Economists are worried by a serious decline in Canada's largest industrial sector: making little ones out of big ones (see graph). The news caused the price of Mr. Juicy futures to fall sharply on international markets last week.

COLUMN

Time to kill, column to fill

BY ALLAN FROTHINGHAM

Zowie, you four-eyed heap of dung beetle droppings, here I am on a seven-and-a-half-hour flight from Europe just trying to mind my own business and you haven't quit breathing all over me since we took off. The stench of smoked almonds and Kaluha emanating from that fetid cakehole of yours is going to make me lose my extruded airline lunch!

Hold still, please. I'm trying to type what you're reading into my lap-top computer.

For God's sake, man, I'm reading the directions on the air-sickness bag!

Can't be helped. Got another column to fill.

If you don't stop breathing on me, I'll...

I once filled a whole back page of **Maclone's** with the installation instructions from a Blaupunkt car stero and passed it off as a commentary on German reunification. No one noticed. Hold the bag still, please.

Woof! Sploosh!!

Peruse me perhaps while I plagiarize the perambulations of your perspicacity ...You know, taking that night school course in alliteration was the smartest career move I ever ... Oh, shtewardess,

make that triples for me and my friend!

Look, you mewling munchkin, if you don't stop drooling on my tie, I'll...

The Jaw that Walks Like a Man, Willy Wooden Shoes, Lotus Land, Ennui on the Rideau—all mine! It's a damn good life, isn't it?

Oh, shut your festering gob!

Not bragging, friend, but I get offered more ass than Fred Davis! I can get all those aspiring young journalistes into all the right parties, you shee...

Is that your tennis racket?

You shtuff, too. Not like Davis... Man, you should shee what goes on backstage when Front Page Challenge hits the road! One time there in Medicine Hat Ol' Pierre got this ...

I'm going to take that racket and I'm going to shove it slowly up your fat ...

Reminds me of the time me 'n Lil Schreyer snuck away from that wretched levee ...

Stewardess! Get me a parachute immediately! I'll give you anything you want.

Shtewardess! A parachute for my friend —and make it a triple.

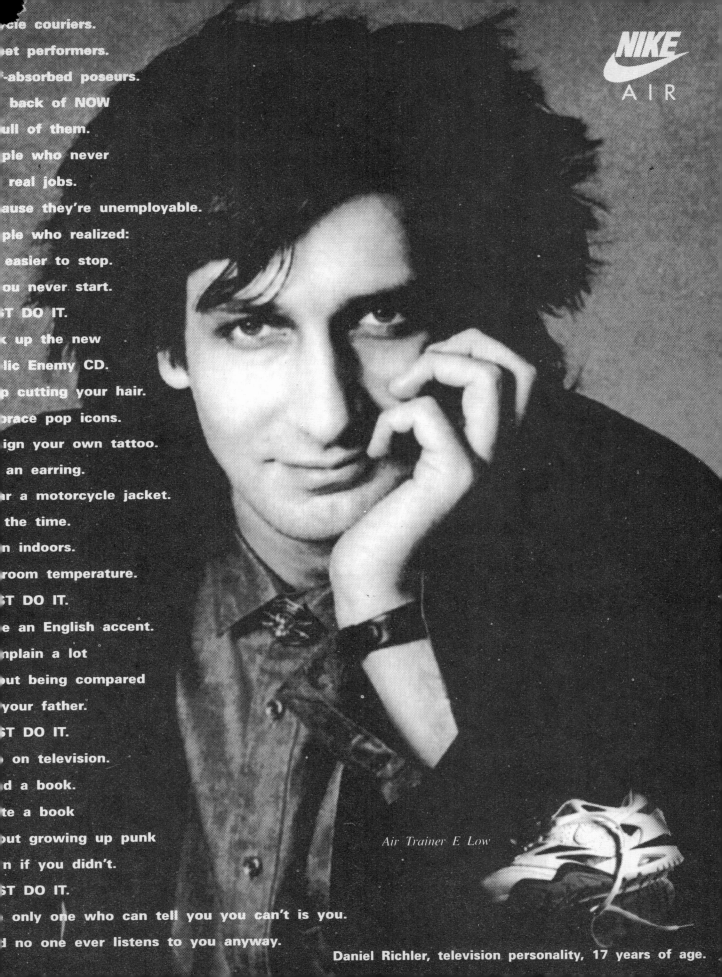

cle couriers.
et performers.
-absorbed poseurs.
back of NOW
ull of them.
ple who never
real jobs.
ause they're unemployable.
ple who realized:
easier to stop.
ou never start.
ST DO IT.
k up the new
lic Enemy CD.
p cutting your hair.
brace pop icons.
ign your own tattoo.
an earring.
r a motorcycle jacket.
the time.
n indoors.
room temperature.
ST DO IT.
e an English accent.
mplain a lot
out being compared
your father.
ST DO IT.
on television.
d a book.
te a book
out growing up punk
n if you didn't.
ST DO IT.
only one who can tell you you can't is you.
d no one ever listens to you anyway.

NIKE
AIR

Air Trainer E Low

Daniel Richler, television personality, 17 years of age.

Dave Nickle's
Inside Report

A Great Canadian Tradition Since Nov. 1983

Vol. XXVII July 14, 1992
© Sloblaw Companies
Ltd. 1992

Unless otherwise stated, prices are effective Sat., July 13 through Sat., Aug. 1, 1992.

David Suzuki's
AMAZING DISCOVERY!

Last month I told you about my horrible plane crash in the Andes, which I managed to survive with the aid of my No-Nation Army Knife, several packets of **Memories of the Donner Pass Meat Tenderizer**, and a number of badly injured economy passengers. What I didn't tell you at the time was the role my seat-mate, the eminent geneticist David Suzuki, played in the survival of the entire first-class section. **NOW IT CAN BE TOLD!** As you know, it's next to impossible to get fresh fruits and vegetables in the An-

des at that time of year. So David went quietly to work on a jar of fruit flies he happened to have in his knapsack. By the end of the week he'd genetically altered them so they resembled big, ripe, juicy beefsteak tomatoes. So delicioso and so easy to swat!

Now, through special licencing arrangements with David, I'm pleased to offer you 500 mL jars of **Suzuki's Own Genetically-Altered Flying Fruit Spaghetti Sauce** at the phenomenally low price of $3.29.

COMING NEXT MONTH
AN ENTIRELY NEW PRODUCT LINE FOR THOSE WHO FIND EVERY CHOICE UNBEARABLE!
SOPHIE'S CHOICE PRODUCTS

GET CRACKING!
POACHED EGGS FOR BEGINNERS!

There's no need to go to some fancy restaurant for poached eggs anymore. Now they're minutes away with my NEW President's Choice Poached Egg Kit ($7.99 a box). INSIDE, YOU'LL FIND TWO MEDIUM EGGS, A CAN OF WATER, A METAL POACHER THINGY, TWO PIECES OF PRE-TOASTED TOAST, A TINY CAN OF STERNO, A MATCH, and an 8-PAGE INSTRUCTION BOOKLET. Voila, in just minutes you'll have delicious poached eggs!

Pickles, 1951-1991

DOGS JUST FINE

This being our 1992 summer barbecue edition, it reminds me that last ye about this time my wife Pickles disappeared. I was meaning to share that w you, but I guess it must have slipped my mind, what with all the internatio outcry over my **Memories of Melbourne Marsupial Marmalade**. I got ba from Birkina Fasso late one night and Pickles and one of the Mercedes w gone. Didn't even shut the goddamn garage door! Anyway, my French B Dogs are doing just fine without her, except of course for Monsieur Tap ("Le Petomane"), the one that just died. He was horribly flatulent, towards end.

1 Tonne Cooked Shrimp $6,999.99

NO BRAINER

Anytime you can buy ONE TONNE O FROZEN COOKED SHELLE SHRIMP for only $6,999.99, yo jump at it — It's a No Brainer! At this price, you'd be a fool no to eat shrimp EVERY DAY fo the REST OF YOUR LIFE! predict we'll move super tanke full of these crafty crustacean Either that or our seafood buye Dickie Thon, will be sleeping wit the fishes!! I recently sent Dickie o. to the ocean with a blank cheque and h came back with simply an incredib amount of shrimp. It's everywhere!! Any way, Dickie has been working overtime shelling and de-veining the litt critters. And I'm making them available to you for the amazingly low pric of less than $7,000 a tonne. (Even less if you buy in bulk.) FREE RECIP BOOK, while supplies last.

NEW! *THIRST A THING OF THE PAST*
MEMORIES O
Paraguay Agua Helada

I was down in Paraguay last winter (their summer) visiting some very ol friends at their *finca* west of Concepcion. It was a hot day, dry and dusty. had been watching my hosts Hermann and Klaus put their men throug hand-to-hand combat drills all morning. By noon, I had a thirst that a ha dozen pilseners and a pitcher of martinis didn't even put a dent in. Ove lunch, Hermann and Klaus introduced me to a clear, cold beverage wit clinky lumps floating in it. I'd never seen anything quite like it! It's some thing the locals call *agua helada*. After several glasses, I knew I ha discovered THE PERFECT SUMMERTIME THIRST QUENCHER! I begge Klaus, the more domestic of the two, to share the secret of th super slaker with me. After I agreed to make a small donatio to his favorite cause, Klaus agreed. Now, thanks to Klau I'm able to present my new **President's Choice Memories** Paraguay Agua Helada just in time for the dog days of th Canadian summer. Pick up a six pack today in the partiall frozen beverage section! 6x175 mL bottles at the astound ing price of just $4.99.

I JUST HAD A DUMP BEHIND THE PIANO!

THON GONE

For almost 20 years, Dickie Thon was my head seafood buyer. Granted, he'd made his share of mistakes—his Memories of Exxon Gannets in Oil, his entire Red Tide line of discount mollusks, his Memories of the Saguenay Beluga Burgers, and others too numerous to mention. I could go on and on about this man. But, I won't, except to say he's dead. Just as we were going to ~~ess~~, the police pulled his wrinkled body from Toronto Harbour. He had been ~~tured~~. I flew back from Ulan Bator the moment I heard he was gone. Very few ~~pe~~ople knew that Dickie played a better-than-average bassoon. He will be ~~m~~issed. P.S. DICKIE, WHERE DID YOU LEAVE YOUR STAPLER?

DOGGONE TASTY!

~~W~~oke up in a Chelsea doorway, vomit caked to my rep tie, a monocle where my ~~sp~~ectacles used to be. My wallet was gone and so were the brass buttons on my ~~bl~~azer. And then it slowly came back to me. Three months earlier I'd been in a ~~litt~~le restaurant in the back streets of Ho Chi Minh City celebrating Tet with the ~~lo~~cals. Naturally, I ordered the most expensive item on the menu, a hearty, ~~ar~~omatic stew. I asked the owner what was in it, and he said it was "thit cay," ~~wh~~ich was Greek to me. He kept pointing at a cage over by the abacus that held

THE FILIPINO HOUSE BOY HASN'T BEEN PAID IN MONTHS!

two mangy mongrels, as if he expected me to share my meal with them. I gave him a handful of Canadian Tire money and left. Later on, back at the hotel, my lovely interpreter Jasmine explained why the restaurateur kept pointing at the dogs. She informed me I'd just eaten an entire schnauser! She said her people simply loved anything doggy-style—poached pit bull, corgi crepes, setter soup, fried beagle brains, Rottweiler ragout, stir-fried Saint Bernard, chihuahua chitlings, Great Danishes... If it barks, they will come—and bring their own chopsticks! I instantly figured if a spavined street cur like the one ~~I~~ just wolfed down could be so tasty, imagine what a pampered kennel-bred ~~C~~anadian puppy would taste like!!! I immediately got on the satellite phone back ~~to~~ Reg at the office, and he phoned this guy he knows down at the pound and... ~~W~~ell, the rest is gourmet history. Just in time for barbecue season, our master ~~b~~utchers have prepared 16 tons of canine just for you. You'll be barking up the ~~ri~~ght taste tree with my **President's Choice Memories of Saigon Frozen Dog** ~~M~~eat. Only $7.79 for a 1 kilo box of assorted poodle or cocker spaniel cuts (no ~~sn~~outs or paws), $7.89 for the delectable French Bull Dog.

PRESIDENT'S CHOICE

~~M~~EMORIES OF UPPER CANADA COLLEGE SHOWER SOAP

~~A~~h, the memory is positively Prous-~~ti~~an! The steam, the smell of chlorine, ~~th~~e squeaky clean feel of hairless flesh! ~~B~~ut most of all it was the scent of the ~~s~~oap the younger boys were forced to ~~m~~ake right in the school kitchen!!! I'll ~~a~~lways remember the first time I acci-~~d~~entally dropped the small shard of ~~s~~oap matron had made me sign for. ~~S~~uddenly, my prefect Pugh Major (and

I do mean major!) brushed against me, and I was dizzy with adolescent delight!

Enough said though. Apparently, there is no statute of limitations on this kind of innocent behaviour. But now you too can relive those first stirrings with my **Memories of Upper Canada College Shower Soap**. Just $1.29 for a 10 g. sliver.

QUADRUPALLY DECADENT!

PRESIDENT'S CHOICE
EXTRA-VIRGIN SAUNA SWEAT

Man, I get a chubby just thinking about this one! There I was just hanging out in Kemi in northern Finland. I was waiting for the limo to come and take me up to Lappland, where I'd been told I could score some primo reindeer meat cheap. Well, the guy who ran the town, the mayor or something, asked me if I wanted to kill some time by taking a sauna with his four teenage daughters. Now, I'd been knocking back the Finlandia all day, and I figured maybe a sauna might be just the ticket. Besides, my blazer needed a good steam....Unfortunately, my lawyers have advised me to skip the part about how I actually discovered the restorative powers of my

quadrupally decadent President's Choice Extra-Virgin Sauna Sweat, at least until we can get the extradition proceedings quashed. But take my word for it, this naturally electrolitic beverage, just ever-so faintly redolent of herring, is pure ambrosia! And I'm offering it at the amazingly low introductory price of $9.99 for a case of 6x750 mL bottles. If you're not completely satisfied, just return it to me and I'll give you your money back and drink it myself.

Damn, it's tasty!

NEW! C'EST SI BON!
NO-NAME JOS. LOUIS-TYPE CAKEY SNACKING UNITS

I couldn't think of any other way to describe them. When I found out the Jos. Louis people move 80 million of these indestructible little units each year, I immediately wanted a piece of the action. They're imported from *la belle province* (Quebec), where the colorful *habitants* often eat them three meals a day!

Only $19.99 a gross. Delicious when washed down with a No-Name Pepsi-Like Cola Beverage!

SUMMER SIZZLE

PRESIDENT'S CHOICE **MEMORIES OF KHARTOUM** Ashtray Sand 5 kg bag only	**$4.99**
PRESIDENT'S CHOICE **DE-ALCOHOLIZED GIN** one litre jug only	**$1.98**
Memories of Bangkok **$9.95** **BULK PENICILLIN** 500 tablets bottle	Buy in bulk and save! **PRESIDENT's CHOICE** **SPANISH FLY** 10 kg bag **$199.50**

A FRANK SERIAL EXCLUSIVE

Excerpted from The Wisdom of the Elders, David Suzuki in conversation with Albert Einstein, prominent dead white European male, and George Muskrat Fart, chief of the Bingo first nation and owner of the Wee-oh-hoo-hee (Ojibway for "Big Long Indian-sounding word") Bait Shop and Yamaha franchise on Lake Simcoe.

David Suzuki: In this modern society, in which people are allowed to do anything they want, it is gratifying that some of us, at least, still follow the ancient trails of the jumbojets, from media opportunity to media opportunity, leaving nothing behind us but our video cassettes and coffee table books. Tell me, oh Chief Muskrat Fart, in what manner do you follow the old ways of wisdom?

Chief Muskrat Fart: 'Have-um 1972 Skidoo. Still runs good. Needed new ignition wires in '87, that all.

DS: But tell us about the joys of huddling for shelter under a pile of leaves and skins. Tell us about the spirituality of a 60 per cent infant mortality rate. What about dressing up in greasy hides and standing for hours in a bug-infested swamp to club some dumb animal to death?

MF: That O. K. Tourist season only from June to September. Go to Bahamas in November.

DS: And the indigenous tradition of floundering through knee-deep muskeg, armed with a rock tied to the end of a stick, and coming between a mother grizzly bear with PMS and her cubs?

MF: You need-um heap-big Yamaha Mudcat 4800 ATV. Four-wheel drive and heap-big independent floating suspension, 170 horse-power. Take no shit from bear. On sale now. 20 per cent off.

Albert Einstein: Excuse me, but considering that an adult grizzly weighs about 1400 kg even with der substantial motorized vehicle, especially if it has no roof, der putative aboriginal driver vud nevertheless be in considerable danger, vud he not?

MF: Heap-big gun rack right behind you, Jack! Standard on Mudcat 5200, optional on 4800. Me throw in for free, you buy heap-big 4800. We make-um deal.

DS: And don't forget the pleasures of starving to death, premature osteoarthritis and a 35-

WISDOM of the ELDERS

PETER KNUDTSON & DAVID SUZUKI

year life expectancy!

MF: No life expectancy for bear with .303 slug up the bung-hole. Heap-big floor rug.

AE: Vas ist dis large heap you mentioning constantly?

MF: That's just a mannerism we use when talking to anthropologists, journalists and anyone wearing negative-heel flip-flops. Actually, there's a question I've always wanted to ask you.

AE: Ja?

MF: O. K., like, you've got these two twins, eh. One gets in a space ship and goes away from Earth at the speed of light for one year and then comes back at the same speed, eh. Because of relativity he'd be a lot younger, eh?

AE: Ja. Assuming instantaneous accelera-

tion, he'd be two years younger than his brother.

DS: And tying people to stakes and pulling their fingernails out! Smoke-induced respiratory diseases! Worshipping the sacred fruit fly god! Think of it! Life without shopping malls! No fast food! No cars!

MF: Yes, but if everything is relative, eh, why can't the twin who stays on Earth be seen as travelling away from the space ship at the speed of light. Then he'd be the younger one, eh?

AE: Ah, but you have forgotten to consider the effect of...

DS: No roads! No plumbing! No sofas! No television! No video cassettes! No coffee-table books! No nature shows!...er...what I meant to say is...

CANADIAN FAIRY TALES PRESENTS:
LITTLE RED RIDING HOOD

CORRECTED BY

MICHELE LANDSBERG
AND DAVID SUZUKI

ONCE UPON A TIME...
A YOUNG WOMAN FINISHED HER SHIFT AT THE ABORTION CLINIC AND STARTED OUT TO VISIT HER GRANDMOTHER TO MAKE SURE THAT SHE WAS NOT BEING ABUSED. SUDDENLY!

SHE CAME ACROSS A BIG MORALLY NEUTRAL WOLF BUT SHE WASN'T AFRAID BECAUSE SHE KNEW THAT WOLVES POSE NO THREAT TO PEOPLE, UNLESS THEY'RE MALE

OF COURSE, FORTUNATELY SHE REMEMBERED HER STREET-PROOFING TRAINING AND CALLED THE RAPE CONTROL CENTRE WHICH ADDED THE WOLF'S NAME TO THE SEX OFFENDER LIST. WHICH WAS TOTALLY UNNECESSARY,

BECAUSE WOLVES ONLY PREY ON THE SICK AND THE OLD, THEREBY CULLING THE MOST UNFIT ANIMALS. LIKE THE GRANDMOTHER? WELL, SHE'S NO LONGER BREEDING AND SHE DOESN'T CONTRIBUTE TO THE GENETIC POOL... YOU WOULDN'T SAY

THAT IF SHE WERE MALE! YOU SEE, IT'S ALL IN THE BALANCE OF NATURE RIGHT! TELL ME ALL ABOUT IT MR. PATRIARCH! COMPETE! KILL! CONSUME! WELL, IF WE ALL CONSUMED LIKE YOU, THE WORLD

ECO-SYSTEM WOULD COLLAPSE IN TWO WEEKS. ANYWAY, WHEN LITTLE RED RIDING HOOD ARRIVED AT HER GRAND- MOTHER'S, SHE WASN'T HOME. PERHAPS SHE WAS IMBIBING THE WISDOM OF THE ELDERS IN A NEARBY SWAMP OR STUDYING SELF DEFENCE TECHNIQUES

BINGO

TO PROTECT HERSELF FROM MALE VIOLENCE? KNITTING WHALE COZYS FOR GREENPEACE? TAKING LESBIAN LESSONS AT NIGHT SCHOOL? RECYCLING HER EAR WAX? BEING DATE RAPED BY HER GERONTOLOGIST? FIGHTING GLOBAL WARMING BY STAYING NUDE? STOP LOOKING AT ME LIKE THAT!

I KNOW WHAT YOU WANT! ALL YOU MEN WANT THE SAME THING! BUT MICHELE! BE FAIR! STOP IT! ZERO TOLERANCE! BUT YOU GET THE FRONT PAGE ALL THE TIME AND I'M ALWAYS IN THE BACK ON SOME CRAPPY SCIENCE PAGE. NO MEANS NO! I WRITE ABOUT THE END OF THE WORLD AND YOU BABBLE ON AND ON ABOUT MALE HORMONES. SURELY, I SHOULD...

GET YOUR HANDS OFF MY COLUMN! AH! THE BRAVE HUNTSPERSON HAS ARRIVED AT GRANDMOTHER'S TO SHOOT THAT DISGUSTING WOLF! NO! HE'S GOING TO SHOOT LITTLE RED RIDING HOOD, AFTER ALL, SHE'S PROBABLY ANNOYING THE WOLF. VIOLENCE AGAINST WOMEN! INDISCRIMINATE WILDLIFE EXTINCTION! MACHO KILLER!

MACHO KILLER!... MICHELE?...ARE YOU THINKING WHAT I'M... YES DAVID YES! THAT IT'S OK WITH YOU IF THE SO-CALLED BRAVE HUNTSPERSON... OH YES DAVID! SHOOTS HIMSELF?... RIGHT IN HIS MALE HORMONE!

NOW... WHAT ABOUT THE OTHER TWO? THEY BOTH LIVE HAPPILY EVER AFTER IN A SUITABLY NON-TRADITIONAL FAMILY POSITIVE ROLE MODEL UNIT. CULLING THE OLD AND SICK! YES, UNTIL HE MURDERS HER IN A HORMONE DRENCHED SEX-FRENZY...OR UNTIL THE INEVITABLE WORLD-WIDE ECOLOGICAL... THE END (PLEASE!)

FRANK *T.V.*

BOB

DIAL *and* DONATE
TELETHON
ONTARIO

—6:00 a.m.—
23 31 Hammy Hamster
A former sheriff adjusts to life in a cage.

—7:30 am—
23 31 Welcome to Pooh Corner
An aging Christopher Robin buys his first 12-pack of Depends.

—8:00 am—
4 6 Under the Umbrella Tree
Holly is visited by the health department after neighbors complain about the stench coming from her apartment.
11 Sharon, Lois & Bram Stoker's Vampire Show
25 Celebrity Croquinole
Semi-final match: Murray Westgate vs. Al Waxman.

—9:00 am—
18 Mister Rogers
Mister Rogers talks the CRTC into issuing him yet another license to print money.
11 Mr. Dressup
Guest: Max Keeping.

—11:00 am—
21 24 You Can't Do That on Television
Les Lye performs frottage on Abby Hagyard.

—11:30 a.m.—
5 Teenage Mutant Ninja Tories
11 De Jong and de Restless
Simon blows his chances of impressing the babes at a political convention when he's found in a compromising position with Mike.
24 Prisoners of Gravity
Scheduled: Pat Carney, Steve Paproski.

—12:00 p.m.—
6 Hull High
After consuming a case of Brador and two large orders of poutine, Louis dies.

—12:30 p.m.—
5 Who's the Boss?
Imelda criticizes Byron's decision to apply the GST to haute couture fashions.
28 Don Cherry's

Grapevine
Don discusses the use of the pluperfect subjunctive with baseball author George F. Will.

—1:30 p.m.—
4 6 On the Road Again
A Newfoundland priest who collects belly-button lint; an ambulatory schizophrenic who lives in a Saskatchewan badger hole; host Wayne Ronstad sings a maudlin, if tunelessly familiar, song.

—2:30 p.m.—
4 6 Meechcombers
The adventures of a fun-loving firm of constitutional lawyers.
6 Simpsons
Jeff annoys the rest of the family by saying "Don't have a cow, man" in Latin.
5 Cosby Show
Denise notices she's a different color from the rest of the Huxtables; Theo becomes a crack addict.
10 Unsolved

Mysteries
Scheduled: How Erica Ehm finds her way to work; CBC sitcoms; Fergie Olver.

—3:00 p.m.—
4 6 Wonder Bread Years
Kevin begins to worry about the hair growing on the palm of his right hand.
6 Canada's Least Wanted
Profiles of Byron Muldoon and Jean Chretien.
13 Romania's Funniest Home Videos
The army stages a mock execution—of a dead man!

—3:30 p.m.—
4 6 Vanelli Boys
Gino tries to hide the scratches on his black car from a prospective buyer.

—4:00 p.m.—
4 6 Street Beagle
Leon discovers he's been neutered; Olivia gets licked in court; Carrie is hit by a garbage truck, while

chasing an ambulance.
6 Fop Rock
The musical lives and loves of San Francisco hair stylists. A Steven Butcho production.
13 In the Heat of the Night Heat
Two southern Ontario cops, one with mousy brown hair, the other with sandy brown hair, put aside their differences to solve crimes.
11 Roseanne
Dan moves into the spare bedroom for obvious reasons.
29 Movie
****"Beverly Sills, Cop" (1986, Musical) Armed only with a Wagner aria, an opera singer-turned-cop blows away a cocaine cartel.
13 Movie
1/2*"Honey, I Expanded the Senate" (1990, Farce) Byron Muldoon, Imelda Muldoon.

—5:00 p.m.—
4 6 Reclining Women
Guest star: Elizabeth Manley.

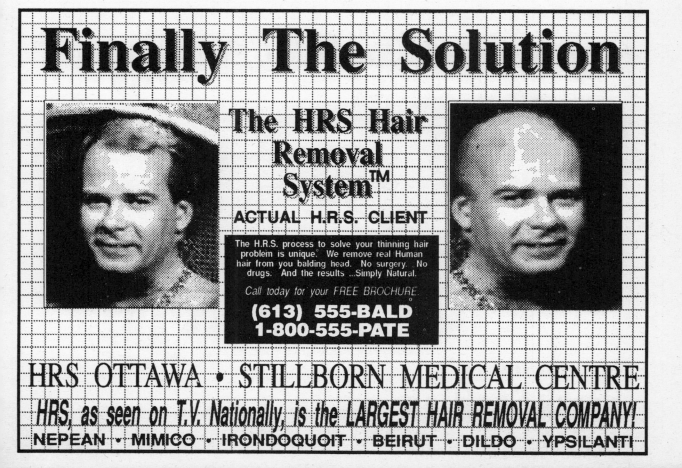

——5:30 p.m.——

2 Polka Dot Door Jim Morrison is stricken with chicken pox.

7 9 16 The New Adventures of Winnie the Zulu Winnie starts a soccer club to teach the neighborhood boys all about headers, hand balls and free kicks.

8 20 34 Fred Pennis's Place Fred shows kids how to make bushel-size servings of popcorn smothered with melted narwhal fat; also, how to weld broken bedframes.

17 NW Spicer's Travelling Reptile Show

28 TSN PTA Golf Parents vs teachers. (R)

——6:00 p.m.——

2 The Skids of De-Greasy Street A rash of automobile accidents near a school sparks a discussion of teenage pregnancy, AIDS, the rain forest, whales, frottage, and nuclear power.

4 Wayne Newton's Apple Wayne and his bodyguards demonstrate

spread sheets.

17 NW Loonie Tunes Bank of Canada governor John Crow explains his monetary policy.

28 TSN Ladies Curling Guest: Farrah Fawcett.

FC Movie ★1/2: "When Larry Met Wally" (Comedy-drama, 1988) Tony Dow, Jerry Mathers. A middle-aged Wally Cleaver finally admits to himself that the love of his life has always been Larry Mondello. (1:56)

——7:00 p.m.——

6 8 16 Walt Disney Resents Tonight's gripe: being dead.

27 MM Vest Pattern Guest Don Cherry demonstrates the moiré effect while reviewing the career of ABBA.

——7:30 p.m.——

3 Copps Real-life drama follows a perky young politician as she gets her hair done at The Bay.

7 This Land B.C. supreme court Judge Allan MacEachern explains

whose land this land really is.

8 20 34 Front Page Challenger A faulty pacemaker causes the world's oldest panel show to explode, killing all aboard, including mystery guest Eugene Forsey.

13 Molson Golden Girls Rose spends the night in the drunk tank; Dorothy discovers she has cirrhosis.

17 NW New Kids in the Centre Block A look at how the men who swapped their integrity and self-respect for a cushy Senate sinecure during the GST debate are coping with the shame and stench.

——8:00 p.m.——

6 8 The Quirks of Adrienne Quarkson (Debut) In the wake of budget cuts, the CBC has decided to combine arts and science programming. Tonight: Gerhard Herzberg sings Kurt Weill; David Suzuki pres-

ents "Noh Theatre for Fruit Flies."

7 16 20 America's Funniest Home Remedies Tonight: Cherry bombs as a cure for hemorrhoids.

9 The Crosbie Show While on a trade deal to Mexico, John loses his watch, his wallet, his passport, his lunch, his pants and our shirt.

28 TSN Canadian Pocket Pool Championships Eugene Forsey vs K.C. Irving. (R)

FC Movie ★ "Drugstore Doughboy" (1990, Farce) Byron Muldoon, Joe Who. Two bumbling frostbacks are tricked into joining the U.S. Marine Corps and going to war. (1:51)

43 50 I Shove Lucy A mediocre Cuban bandleader is deported after being convicted of wife abuse.

——8:30——

7 Head in the Class Father Bill is arrested.

8 19 20 43 50 The Donder Years Dancer and Prancer leave the team to become florists; Donder head-butts Rudolph to death and assumes leadership of the entire North Pole.

21 YTV 24 Deke Wilson After bringing down a new budget, Deke is forced to send his wife to live in the United States so he can afford her cigarette habit.

——9:00 p.m.——

2 Colombo Columnist Allan Fotheringham is forced to sue himself for plagiarism when Colombo includes him in a new collection of quotations.

6 8 The Nature of Thingies Guest: Elizabeth Manley.

7 Unsolved Mysteries Byron Muldoon, a man who couldn't win a popularity contest in his own bed, inexplicably serves two terms as prime minister of what used to be Canada.

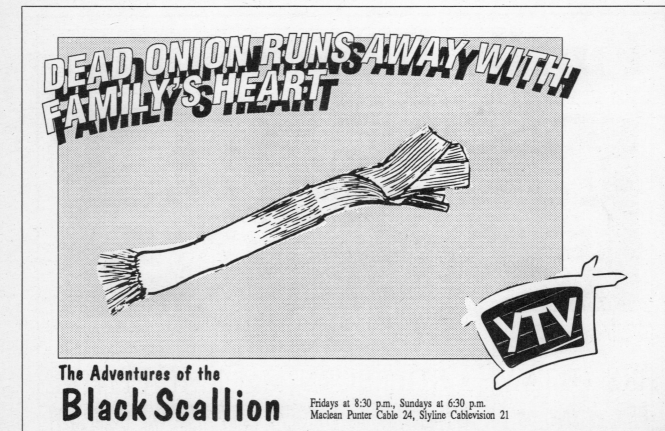

13 Movie 1/2★ "George Bush Hail, Hail Iraq 'n' Oil" (1991, Made for TV) George Bush, Norman Shwarzkopf. A man shakes the wimp tag by engineering the killing of tens of thousands of innocent people.

16 Movie ★ "Postbusters" (1986, Horror-Comedy) Donald Lander. A mad financial wizard finds a way to rip the remaining vestiges of community out of small-town Canada. (2:00)

14 VIS30 Firestone Theatre A man convinces a small town he can put them in the big leagues if only they'll give him a big parcel of land and all their loose change.

28 TSN Mini-Rumble in the Jungle Professional miniature golf tour. Live from Zaire, the Gary Coleman Pgymy Open.

——10:00 p.m.——

2 Pawprint Host Spaniel Richler sniffs out Michael J. Fox's biographer Michael Corgi.

6 Beverly Sills, 90210 Beverly puts on so much weight she's assigned a zip code.

7 16 20 Peon Rider Tired of picking coffee beans for three pesos a month, Juan Valdez and his faithful burro Exxon try their hand at cocaine smuggling.

28 TSN Prisoners of Gravity Quarter-final match: Mike Puffy vs Michael Coren.

A&E Delvecchio When Alex screws up a two-on-one, Gordie gives him an elbow in the head.

FC Movie 1/2 ★ "Soiled Green" (Farce, 1991) Robert de Cotret, Byron Muldoon. A horribly polluted society of the future exists on a synthetic food made from worthless campaign promises (1:46)

——10:22 p.m.——

6 8 19 20 43 50 Frum Hair...To Eternity In an effort to finally set the country straight on Meech Lake, multiculturalism, Israel, the Gulf War and much-maligned property developers, Barbara is forced to interview herself.

——10:30 p.m.——

13 Elderly Queen (Debut) A blue-haired detective (Quentin Crisp) solves "The Mystery of the Comatose Gerbil."

——11:00 p.m.——

A&E Singh Singh A look inside a notorious Sikh prison.

27 MM Blue Spotlight Special Don Cherry's dog performs "I Lick It 'Cause I Can" with guest Ellen Barkin.

——11:30 p.m.——

6 16 20 Arsenio Hole Arsenio fawns himself to death, whereupon his body is ripped to pieces and eaten by his adoring audience.

8 Cinema ★ "Crocodile Muldoon II" (1990, Comedy) Byron Muldoon, Gérard Veilleux. The boy from Baie Comeau is back to show those ingrates at the public broadcasting network what a really big knife looks like. (1:48)

9 George Michael's Sex Machine All the latest cricket and association football scores, plus George sings "I Want Your Shorts."

28 TSN All-Ireland Bomb-Planting Championship: Semi-finals (Location to be announced)

——12:00 a.m.——

13 Paid Program MuchMusic VJ Erica Uhm gets her bikini line done. (4:00)

19 Movie ★ "The Thief of Baghdad" (Murder mystery, 1990) Saddam Insein, Madame Insein. An eastern potentate makes the tragic error of taking the United States literally. (2:20)

14 VIS30 Ed Van Impe Was Fred Shero the Antichrist?; is Mario Lemieux's sweater number two-thirds predicted in the Book of Revelations?; playing it one Armageddon at a time.

28 TSN Monster Ego Wreck 'Em Race Bobby Campeau vs Donny Trump.

FC Movie ★★★★ "Her Alibi" (Romance, 1990) Christoper Plumber, Imelda Muldoon. (2:09)

6 16 20 Movie ★★ "The Silence of the Hams" (Horror, 1991) Mike Puffy, Leigh Cathedral. A pair of newspersons is drawn together when they each must find a cure for their chronic flatulence or lose their jobs. (1:54)

8 Cisco and Ebert The Cisco Kid and Roger Ebert review this week's move releases, including "The Duncan Renaldo Story" and "Leo," a musical based on the life of the great Mexican actor Leo Carrillo.

⒀ Twin Beaks
Larry Zolf shares donuts and coffee with Dr. Henry Morgentaler.

⑪ thirtysomething
Hope resents Michael's new modem; Nancy and Elliot agonize over new sheets.

— 12:30 a.m. —

④ ⑥ Santa Barbara Frum
Not a guest tonight or ever: Fabulously wealthy best-selling right-wing loony author Claire Ahoy.

— 1:00 a.m. —

⑪ Arsenio Hole
Scheduled: Gary Coleman talks about his life as a pathetic, pistol-packing, two-foot skinhead; Arsenio sucks up to some brainless white movie bimbo.

㉓ ㉛ Rocco and Mowinckel
Animated. An interior decorator finds happiness with an Italian goat herd after fleeing Canada to avoid bad debts and tasteless clients.

— 2:00 a.m. —

④ Magnum, P.E.I.
Magnum is pursued by a henna-rinsed alcoholic floozy who claims she's Anne Shirley.

⑥ Movie
1/2 * "Tomb of the Living Dead" (1990, Horror) Wilbert Keon, Alan MacEachen.

⒀ Jake and the Fatman
Mike Puffy talks with Jake Epp.

㉑ Home Shopping Club
Jerky pictures of zircon-encrusted Elvis hemorrhoid cushions.

The PUFFSTER

Heh, heh, O.K., what do you *Frank* guys want? Ya, you're right. So there's no *real* contest about Caroline. I made it up for my column.

But, hey, this isn't exactly the first time I've sucked up to power. You guys have to see this great Bill Kempling impersonation I do.

Sheila...I apologize...You slut. **Ha, ha ha, ho, ho** (wheeze) **hee, hee,** (snort).

Wait a minute! You guys set me up! You're mocking me! I'll sue. Your magazine's dead. I'll call MacAdam...I'll talk to Doug...I'll...I'll...

The PUFFSTER

Zzzzzz...Zzzzzzzzz...zzzzzz... snort...Zzzzzz...Zzzzzzz

Oh...hi ya guys. Caught the big guy napping, I'm afraid. Even I sometimes have a hard time staying awake through my show.

You know how it is, a segment on *Canada AM* once a week, a lame public affairs show on Sundays where I get to repeat over and over the same embarrassingly empty thoughts I've already handed in to the *Sun*. Wears a guy out.

Hey...just a minute. You *Frank* jerks are mocking me again. I won't stand for it. When I tell Brian he's gonna...just you wait. I know he's going to the UN, and then you're gonna get what's coming to you. Why I ought to...

The PUFFSTER

Look into my eyes. You are getting sleepy...sleeeepy... sleeeeeeepy. *Sunday Emission* is on. You started dozing at the breakfast table while reading my column in the *Sun*.

Your eyelids weigh down like lead. Your ears fill with cotton. Your mind becomes a comfortable buzz of meaningless but assuring, placating phrases.

When and if you awake, you will feel like a truck ran over your brain as if it were a hesitating rodent. Yet you will not notice. You will not remember the show. You will not learn anything.

But if you have a BBM or Neilson rating book to fill out, go and fill in full family viewing of *Sunday Emission* for all weeks covered. And Brian Mulroney will win the next election.

Good evenin'. Yeah, it's me, an' I'm sittin' in tonight for this Pete Mansbridge fella who's at home tonight 'cause he's all outa joint about gettin' his little schedule shuffled around durin' the playoffs...

...Well, let me tell ya, pouty Petey, I didn't expect this kinda no-show cheapshot from no Canadian newsreader—maybe some chicken Swede wanna drive around in his Vulvo shoppin' for furniture you gotta put together yourself or sumpin'.

...Okay, news 'n'stuff. All ya bleedin' heart pacifists out there, this is the 'xample what happen when ya don't allow no fightin'. Okay, roll the tape, take a look at this...

...the PM gets a peace pipe up his nose. So I'm thinkin', what woulda happen if it were Stan Jonathan, scrappy little aboriginal guy we had on the Bruins? He wouldn'ta shoved no peace pipe up the PM's nose. He woulda pounded the PM's head to pemmican and then he woulda shoved the peace pipe up his ass. An' Probert, big tough psycho, woulda lit it first.

Okay, earthquake somewhere today and some foreigners got killed, no big deal. Gotta win those face-offs in your own end, amigos.

...Lets take a look at it on the telestrater. Ya see, ya got a big epicene there in Limon. What kind of name for a place is Limon. Sounds more like a fruit. Nobody wants to come from no place named after a fruit. Belleville—now there's a name for a town. Ya don't see no earthquakes in Belleville...

...same thing with, this Manning guy — Prestone. What kind of a name is Prestone, anyways? Sounds like sumpin' you put in your rad on a cold day...

...Take a look on the replay. Ya see ya get a guy like this sittin' on his butt behind a desk all day and look at him—he looks like he never seen a chair before...

Like they got this little problem in Israel with all them Russians they got comin' in there. Comin' over and takin' jobs an' housin' from those Israeli kids, just like the NHL's lettin' them take jobs away from good Canadian boys.

And you see the stick work those Russians lay on like Fetisov clips Coffey inna face. Send Mathieu Schneider over there and straighten things out. Good tough Jewish kid....

Like in Turkey—what a dumb name for a country. Don't get no respect when ya go 'round callin' yourself Turkey. Gotta change that, you Turkey guys out there. Sounds like all nicey-nice Miss Muffet time 'cause the Curds are still gettin' in the whey. Send Marty McSorley over there, straighten that...[CLICK]

1. Museum of Caricature

At first they were kind of cute, but then they got under everyone's skin. Cartoonists. Like Aislin, Peterson, and Larter. Even Macpherson. So we gave them a sweet deal. Their own museum, with a guaranteed market for their "art," and an annual free meal. But it didn't work. The cartoons kept coming. Can't these people take a bribe?! Good fun, anyway. Stumble by in the Byward Market, and find it if you can. Special Exhibition: Byron–No Whore like an Old Whore.

Hours: 9:00 to 7:30

Admission: Ben Wicks isn't funny.

2. National Press Club

If you get into town early, you may want to check out the media watering hole. But by the weekend it'll be empty as most of "the boys" stumble through the hospitality suites looking for "stories." But before the convention, stop on by, and shake Puffy or Gratton by the hand. Tell 'em The Boss sent you.

Happy Hour: You've got to be kidding.

Admission: Hey, I bought the last round!

3. Nate's Deli

Heh, heh, a bit of fun for the Tory with a sense of irony, and a penchant for good ole diner food. Glen Kealey nearly brought down the government here. Bask in the early, freewheeling atmosphere of the green days in power. Tell 'em you'll have what Roch Lasalle is having...but only if you've got a good lawyer.

4. Bank of Canada

Financial epicentre of the nation, and home to our man in the vault, John Crow. Don't miss the special Friday event in the courtyard--the Miss Wrestle Inflation to the Ground contest.

5. National Arts Centre Restaurant

(Caterer to Imelda Muldoon)

Stop by and have a snack, Mila does. Or a case of wine, some china, a jar of caviar, and some nifty table centers. Don't worry about the bill, Denis got it.

6. 50 O'Connor Street

Nice enough building, but why do you want to go in there?

7. Parliament Hill

The prize we're all here for. Come by and check out the inspiring Gothic

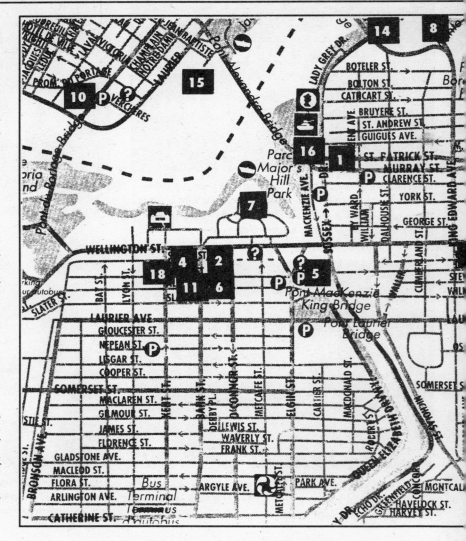

TORY SLEAZE

stonework, the majesty of democratic government, and 50 metre zone exclusion for weirdos, freaks, and other malcontents. A gentle reminder, though. No farting in the Centennial fountain. Accidents do happen.

8. Government House

The best way to rob a bank is by owning one, and that's the same philosophy our party has when it comes to constitutional monarchy. Try making the Governor-Generalship a dumping ground for wildly

partisan but, alas, defeated Tory candidates. We did, and if that hasn't taken 10 years off the life of our constitution, then nothing will.

Special Event: Tea with Ray and Gerda.

Admission: Free of Gravitas

The grounds are open. The attire is formal but empty.

9. RCMP HQ

A Mountie always gets his man, but usually not until after election day. Not only do these folks look good standing outside

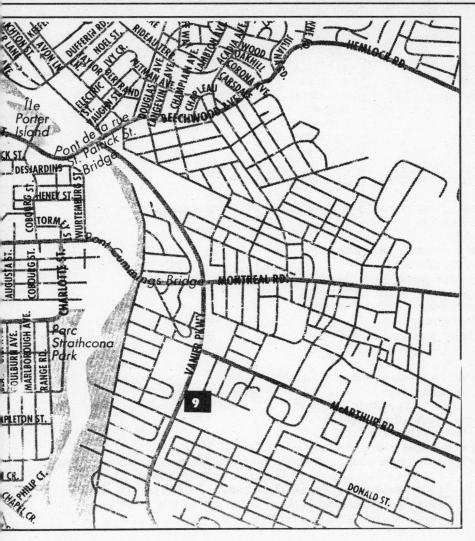

DE TO OTTAWA

of the parole board positions we're drawing for through the weekend.

12. Lincoln Memorial
Not yet.

13. Canada Post Headquarters
The lights are low. The grids and monitors are an electronic duplicate of our nation's lifeblood. An alarm brings a knot of white coated technicians into an impromptu conference around a small display. Caught another Postie peeing without lifting the seat in Postal Station B, Toronto. And you were there to see it! Hours: 1100 to 1300.
Admission: We give untendered contracts, and bully our auditors.

14. 24 Sussex
The lights are on, but nobody's home. Honestly. They're up at Harrington Lake. But make friends with a Mountie, and maybe you can get a peek inside. You're right, it is gutted. Don't worry about the furniture. It's, ah, in storage. Yeah, that's right, in storage.
Hours: Closed to the public. Available for private parties.
Admission: It was all Trudeau's fault.

15. Museum of Criminalization
Michel Cogger's fascinating collection of contracting deals and lame cultural history. Worth a visit, but only if completely hammered, when you can sing "It's a Small World" as many times as you can before the cops arrive.
Ours: Not yours.
Admission: 5% upfront (You're still in Hull, remember.)

16. National Gallery
No receptions or parties planned for us in the Great Hall. The rest is full of art stuff, so we recommend giving it a miss.

17. CBC
Been there. Done that. Got the T-shirt. Stacked the board of directors and executive suites.
Hours: Repositioned
Admission: This is a sacred trust which we share with all Canadians...etc., etc.

18. Holt Renfrew
Where Imelda runs up big bills.

doorways, but they take orders pretty well, too. Have a glance around, and say a silent prayer. Remember to ask about the current status of any number of ongoing MP investigations–the Force's forgotten musical ride.
Special Exhibition: Henry Jensen Collection 0900-1730 hrs.
Admission: Of responsibility not required.

10. Hull
Welcome to the Michel Gravel theme park. Enough said. But do check out Andre Bissonette's Chicken Coop for the best table dancing in town. And don't forget the Lido and the Lipstick.
Wings: 10 cents a piece.
Arms: $250 a fracture.
Admission: 5% upfront.
Secondary Admission: Not Guilty. OK, Guilty.

11. Hy's Steak House
The salon and millworks of our Party. Stop by for meat and potatoes...and one

The Frank Redress Application Form

Dear Frank,

I hereby object in the strongest possible terms to your story _____ *(give title)* in Frank # ____ *(edition)*, wherein you referred to ☐ me   ☐ my mother   ☐ my gerbil as *(check one from column A and one from column B)* a/an...

A
- ☐ bovaristic
- ☐ dasypygal
- ☐ duck-lipped
- ☐ gnathonic
- ☐ gormless
- ☐ oleaginous
- ☐ rebarbative
- ☐ other _____

(please specify)

B
- ☐ archdeacon
- ☐ dominatrix
- ☐ fancy skater
- ☐ financier
- ☐ headmaster
- ☐ bingo caller
- ☐ young Tory
- ☐ other_____

(please specify)

and, further, falsely depicted ☐ me ☐ my mother ☐ my gerbil as (check as many as applicable) a/an...
- ☐ trampoline artiste
- ☐ avid pianist
- ☐ seducer of secretaries and widows
- ☐ lovely AND intelligent
- ☐ other *(please specify)* _____.

I forthwith demand...
- ☐ a complete and unequivocal retraction
- ☐ grovelling apology
- ☐ a duel to the death
- ☐ a date.

If I do not obtain immediate satisfaction I will have no recourse but to...
- ☐ cancel my subscription
- ☐ cancel my mother's subscription
- ☐ cancel my gerbil's subscription
- ☐ release the video tapes
- ☐ file suit for damages in a court of law.
  (If latter option selected, please indicate the amount of damages you will be seeking)
  - ☐ an amount equal to Imelda Muldoon's AmEx balance
  - ☐ the Gross National Product of the Benelux Nations
  - ☐ the value of a Quebec publisher's Nazi memorabilia collection
  - ☐ dinner for two at the Red Lobster.

I hereby state that I am over 21 and not engaged in entrapment.

Sincerely,

- ☐ Peter Mansbridge etc., etc.
- ☐ Other _____
  (please specify)

I enclose a cheque or money order (no stamps please) for $999.98 to cover handling, shredding, and disposal.

Personal Information of Claimant. For office use only.

Age: _____

Sex:
- ☐ Male
- ☐ Female
- ☐ Tory
- ☐ Waiting for elective surgery
- ☐ Negotiable.

Education: ☐ Dalhousie Law School
☐ Ashbury

Marital status:
- ☐ We're seeing a counsellor
- ☐ "Single"
- ☐ Other woman
- ☐ Other man
- ☐ Friend of His Worship
- ☐ Expecting a litter
- ☐ Liz Manley fiance
  (If latter, please give date, location, and duration _____.)

FINANCIAL TIMES

CIRCULATION: YES

Another yawner about wood, pulp and paper

By T.H.E. Lorax
Tree correspondent

IT'S a real snoozer about softwood lumber imports. Yawn. We've seen this before. Extremely flat stuff. Nothing of any real interest to you. Frankly, I wouldn't have made it this far. No, I'd be digging through the back pages looking for breakfast cereal ads. Duties, tariffs, reforestation, pulp and paper—heard it all before.

Right. Let's carry on. What is softwood lumber and why do I care about it? Why don't we hear about hardwood lumber? I mean wood, relatively speaking, is a fairly rigid material, isn't it? See, I'm still not interested. Nothing absorbing to be found in this piece. Move on. Really, I mean it.

MONEY MARKETS
This one is tedious

If you thought the lead story was dull, take a look at this crasher. It's really awful stuff. Bland is the word that comes to mind. Completely void of anything interesting or novel. Christ, this is a dry read.
SEE PAGE 78

Terribly dry bit about the Japanese stock market

By Saduharo Oh
Our man in Tokyo

THIS one is really dull. Tremendously dull, in fact. A very stale story about the Japanese stock market dropping like a stone. Really tedious stuff here. Not at all worth bothering to read. Say, what's the Yen worth anyway? And how do they get those neat little Yen signs on WordPerfect—you know, the upside-down teepees with the line across them? ¥. Right, that's the one.

If I were you, I'd have moved on to something else after the last paragraph. Oh, here are some fascinating numbers: 16 basis points, 51% share, 1.2 million units. That was exciting wasn't it? Me, I've got chills.

Maybe if we threw in a picture of some terminal old Jap it might give this thing some spice, but I doubt it. No, there's no salvaging this baby. It's a yawner, through and through. Relentlessly unexciting. How can we write this stuff, day after day, week after week, month after month, year after year? It just goes on and on. Never ceasing. An infinite abyss of grayness.

How could this one posssibly be any duller?

By Ivan Reitman
No relation

ALRIGHT, here's one with a glimmer of promise. The Reichmanns. Yes, I've heard of them. Obscenely wealthy fellows with beards. Into real estate, aren't they? So they're losing their shirts, eh? Well, that's fitting isn't it. Sue those poor clowns at Toronto Life into the ground and you're bound to reap some bad karma along the way.

But still, this isn't exactly scintillating stuff. No dynamic personalities at work here. Nothing like that Trump fellow and his babes. I wonder if the Reichmanns get any action. Probably.

Okay, back to it. Olympia and York and a thing called Canary Wharf. Right. Nice name that Canary Wharf. Sounds like a place I might want to visit if I ever get over to London. Banks are recalling bond issues and the Reichmanns are overextended. Now they're talking about debt restructuring. See, now you've lost me again. Sorry, not interested in that business. Do yourself a favour and skip to next bit. Further reading of this drivel will only cause chronic boredom. You are warned. Enough..

Travel

Iraq: Land of Contrasts

By Marjorie Fielding Mellish
Special Correspondent

BAGHDAD—After all the romance and excitement of Liberia, Harold and I were looking forward to a relaxing time in rustic Baghdad. Thus far, it is not as relaxing as we had envisioned, but I am sure we shan't come home disappointed.

In fact, we sometimes joke we may not return home at all. Such is the hospitality of the swarthy yet hospitable Iraqi people, to whom we are not mere tourists, but rather honored "guests."

Our sojourn in the Iraqi capital, which dates back to 763 A. D., has been made extremely pleasant by a swarthy Iraqi government official, a Mr. Hussein, who is perhaps from the department of tourism. Mr. Hussein seemed especially delighted to discover that Harold enjoys dual British-American citizenship on account of his father having moved around so much when Harold was a child.

Our first night in exotic Baghdad, at the confluence of the Tigers and Youfraidies Rivers (I will have to delve into my volumes of Sumerian mythology for an explanation of these colorful names, but it is perhaps an earlier version of the Little Black Sambo myth we all enjoyed so much as children), we even appear on Mr. Hussein's television show, which we understand to be the Iraqi version of Big Jim's World, which we used to watch on our community cable channel back home.

Continued on T10

The expansive Iraqi countryside, where locals say you can see bivouaking Screaming Eagles on a clear day.

Mini-Tours cater to tiny travelers

By Tony Lothario
Staff writer

Lilliput Tours Ltd. of Buttonville, Ont. is to be commended for offering a series of package tours this fall aimed at one of the slowest growing travel demographics, namely dwarves, midgets, elves, trolls, jockeys, etc.

Billed as "Big Vacations for Little People," Lilliput offers a 15-day Europe by Mini-van Tour visiting Andorra, Liechtenstein, Luxembourg, Monaco and San Marino. The Nov. 15 tour is $1889 plus departure tax (based on quadruple occupancy). An additional five-day walking tour of the Vatican is also available.

Lilliput also offers a package to PondWorld aquatic theme park in Little Vero Beach, Florida, where vacationers will actually get a chance to frolic with Stinky, PondWorld's fabulous performing smelt. Departures are Nov. 12, 19 and 26.

Other Lilliput packages include a seven-day miniature golfing vacation at the Billy Barty Memorial Mini-putt in Pebble Beach, CA.

And for the outdoorsy half-pint, there's also Lilliput's popular two-

Lilliput Tours proprietor, Eddie Gaedel.

day Shetland Pony Trek up Hamilton's Mount Hope.

Contact: Lilliput Tours, Buttonville, Ont. 416-555-0101

FRANK

Don't leave home without it.

SO LONG SUCKERS!

SOUVENIR RESIGNATION ISSUE

18, 1993 • ISSUE 137 • EVERY TWO WEEKS